World Class

EXPANDING ENGLISH FLUENCY

NANCY DOUGLAS | **JAMES R. MORGAN**

NATIONAL GEOGRAPHIC LEARNING | CENGAGE Learning

Australia • Brazil • Japan • Korea • Mexico • Singapore • Spain • United Kingdom • United States

**World Class: Expanding English Fluency
Student Edition**
Nancy Douglas and James R. Morgan

Publisher: Sherrise Roehr

Managing Editor: Sarah Thérèse Kenney

Development Editors: Michael Poor, Michael Tom

Senior Technology Product Manager: Scott Rule

Technology Project Manager: Chris Conroy

Director of Global Marketing: Ian Martin

Senior Product Marketing Manager: Katie Kelley

Director, Content and Media Production:
  Michael Burggren

Content Project Manager: Andrea Bobotas

Print Buyer: Mary Beth Hennebury

Cover Designer: Cenveo Publisher Services

Cover Image: Chris Brundige

Compositor: Cenveo Publisher Services

Student Book + Student CD-ROM ISBN-13: 978-1-133-56589-5

Student Book + Student CD-ROM ISBN-10: 1-133-56589-1

Student Book + Online Workbook ISBN-13: 978-1-285-06308-9

Student Book + Online Workbook ISBN-10: 1-285-06308-2

National Geographic Learning
20 Channel Center Street
Boston, MA 02210
USA

Cengage Learning is a leading provider of customized learning solutions with office locations around the globe, including Singapore, the United Kingdom, Australia, Mexico, Brazil, and Japan.

Cengage Learning products are represented in Canada by Nelson Education, Ltd.

Visit National Geographic Learning online at **ngl.cengage.com**

Visit our corporate website at **www.cengage.com**

Printed in China
4 5 6 7 8 23 22 21 20 19

Acknowledgements

The authors and editorial team would like to thank the many dedicated instructors who took the time to review World Class. *Their feedback was invaluable during the development of this program.*

UNITED STATES Touria Ghaffari, EC New York, New York, New York; **Olga Gusak,** Computer Systems Institute, Skokie, Illinois; **William Jex,** American Language Institute, New York University, New York, New York; **Bridget McDonald,** Independent Learning Services, Boston, Massachusetts; **Saida Pagan,** North Valley OC, Mission Hills, California; **Tara Tarpey,** American Language Institute, New York University, New York, New York

LATIN AMERICA Luiz Otávio Barros, Associação Alumni, Brazil; **Clarissa Bezerra,** Casa Thomas Jefferson, Brazil; **Isabela Villas Boas,** Casa Thomas Jefferson, Brazil; **Tatiane C. de Carvalho,** Cultura Britânica e Americana, Brazil; **Rafael Reis Carpanez,** Cultura Inglesa, Brazil; **Janette Carvalhinho de Oliveira,** Centro de Linguas - UFES, Brazil; **Samara Camilo Tomé Costa,** IBEU, Brazil; **Frank Couto,** Casa Thomas Jefferson, Brazil; **Denise Santos da Silva,** Associação Cultural Estados Unidos, Brazil; **Marilena Fernandes,** Associação Alumni, Brazil; **Vanessa Ferreira,** Associação Cultural Brasil Estados Unidos, Brazil; **Marcia Ferreira,** CCBEU Franca, Brazil; **Maria Regina Filgueiras,** College Language Center, Brazil; **Maria Righini,** Associação Cultura Inglesa, Brazil; **Bebeth Silva Costa,** Betina's English Course, Brazil; **Domingos Sávio Siqueira,** Federal University of Bahia, Brazil; **Joyce von Söhsten,** English by Joyce von Söhsten, Brazil; **Doris Flores,** Universidad Santo Tomas, Chile; **Sandra Herrera,** Inacap Apoquindo, Chile; **Jair Ayala Zarate,** La Salle University, Colombia; **Rosario Mena,** Instituto Cultural Dominico Americano, Dominican Republic; **Raúl Billini,** Language Program Administration, Dominican Republic; **Rosa Vásquez,** John F. Kennedy Institute of Languages, INC., Dominican Republic; **Elizabeth Ortiz,** COPEI-COPOL English Institute, Ecuador; **José Alonso Gaxiola Soto,** Universidad Autonoma de Sinaloa, Mexico; **María Elena Mesías Ratto,** Universidad de San Martín de Porres, Peru

EUROPE AND THE MIDDLE EAST Juan Irigoyen, International Institute, Spain; **Nashwa Nashaat Sobhy,** San Jorge University, Spain; **Barbara Van der Veer,** International Institute, Spain; **Deborah Wilson,** American University of Sharjah, United Arab Emirates

ASIA Michael Lay, American Intercon Institute, Cambodia; **Kirkland Arizona Kenney,** Beijing New Oriental School, China; **Isao Akama,** Waseda University, Japan; **Benjamin Bailey,** University of Shizuoka, Japan; **James Baldwin,** Tokyo University of Agriculture and Technology, Japan; **Jonathan deHaan,** University of Shizuoka, Japan; **Todd Enslen,** Tohoku University, Japan; **Peter Gray,** Hokusei Gakuen University, Japan; **Linda Hausman,** Gakushuin University, Japan; **Mauro Lo Dico,** Nanzan University, Japan; **Nobue Mori,** Kumamoto Gakuen University, Japan; **Yuri Nishio,** Gifu Pharmaceutical University, Japan; **Geraldine Norris,** The Prefectual University of Shizuoka, Japan; **Christopher Piper,** Takushoku University, Japan; **Michael Radcliffe,** Yokohama City University, Japan; **Jean-Pierre Richard,** Kanagawa University, Sophia University, Japan; **Greg Rouault,** Konan University, Hirao School of Management, Japan; **Stephen Ryan,** Yamagata University, Japan; **Gregory Strong,** Aoyama Gakuin University, Japan; **Michael Yasui,** Tokyo Metropolitan University, Japan; **Sun Mi Ma,** Ajou University, Korea; **Palarak Chaiyo,** Rajamangala University of Technology Suvarnabhumi, Thailand; **Krishna Kosashunhanan,** Thai-Nichai Institute of Technology, Thailand; **Jonee de Leon,** Universal English Center, Vietnam; **Ai Nguyen Huynh Thi,** VUS, Vietnam

We would also like to extend a special thank-you to Yeny Kim for her many insights. Her thoughtful contributions were a great asset and will be felt by students and teachers alike.

READING	WRITING	SPEAKING	VIDEO
What Happens When a Language Dies?: Languages disappearing worldwide **Strategy:** Working with restatement questions	Write a report summary **Strategy:** Writing a report summary	Present your report summary **Strategy:** Interpreting the results and questioning the results	*A Hidden Language Recorded*
Micro Loans, Macro Impact **Strategy:** Determine the meaning of unfamiliar words in a text	Write about advantages and disadvantages	Convince a billionaire investor to loan you money	*Borrowing Money*
Rapid Urbanization: A case study **Strategy:** Locating and reading statistics	Write a summary **Strategy:** Guidelines on summary writing	Talk about push/pull factors that impact migration	*Climate Change Drives Nomads to Cities*
Secrets of the Happiest Places on Earth	Compare and contrast yourself with another person	Take a life satisfaction survey **Strategy:** Making general and specific comparisons	*The Secrets of Long Life*
The Boy with the Amber Necklace: 3,500 years ago, Stonehenge was attracting visitors from all over the world. The question is: Who were they?	Recount a story **Strategy:** Using a graphic organizer to help you tell a story	Explain mysterious places in the world **Strategy:** Refuting a theory	*Discoveries in a Village Near Stonehenge* **Pronunciation:** Differences between American English and British English
Making Mars the New Earth: What would it take to green the red planet, and should we do it?	Write a counterargument **Strategy:** Making a counterargument	Speak for a minute about space exploration	*Profiles in Exploration*

READING	WRITING	SPEAKING	VIDEO
The World Is Our Classroom: Traveler Profile: Michael Palin **Strategy:** Recognizing synonyms	Describe a life lesson **Strategy:** Writing a thesis statement and a conclusion	Sources of learning	*Student Voices on University Rankings*
Celebrity Endorsements: An interview with Ben Anderson, celebrity marketing expert **Strategy:** Summarizing the writer's ideas	Write an opinion piece that contains both facts and opinions **Strategy:** Balancing facts and opinions	Choose the perfect celebrity to endorse your product **Pronunciation:** Intonation to show sarcasm and irony	*In the Spotlight: Kate Middleton*
Nature's Prescription	Write a cause and effect paragraph describing stress factors in your life **Strategy:** Showing cause and effect	Talk about factors that affect your physical and mental well-being	*How Your Brain Handles Stress* **Pronunciation:** Reducing to schwa: high-frequency function words
Majestic Waters	Email for formal communication **Strategy:** Using appropriate register	Discuss how to restore a vacation spot to its former glory	*Jellyfish Lake*
Lost Leonardo: The Palazzo Vecchio is one of Florence's most beautiful public spaces, but its most important masterpiece isn't even there anymore . . . or is it? **Strategy:** Identifying and understanding referents	Write a definition essay **Strategy:** Writing a definition essay	Evaluate different works of art: Are they art? **Pronunciation:** The prominence of stress	*Urban Art: Graffiti*
Comic Relief: The Role of Humor in Society	Write a persuasive essay in support of a nominee for a prize	Tell a funny story using pauses and emphasis **Strategy:** Using pauses and emphasis	*The Immigrant*

World Class 2 Student Book Walkthrough

Explore a Unit

The first half of each unit leads students through guided and communicative practice to master target structures.

Stunning images and thought-provoking questions encourage learners to **think critically** about the unit theme.

Clearly stated **Unit Outcomes** provide a roadmap of learning for the student.

Relevant, high frequency vocabulary is practiced in contextualized exercises.

The **Grammar** section allows learners to refine their grammar skills and practice the grammar through first controlled and then open-ended activities.

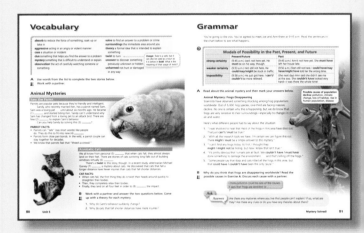

Listening activities encourage learners to listen for and consolidate key information, reinforcing the language, and allowing learners to personalize and think critically about the information they hear.

The **Connections** section allows learners to synthesize the vocabulary and grammar they have learned through personalized communication.

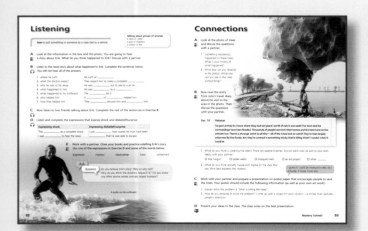

The second half of the unit focuses on skill-building and communication. The strands build on one another with a final communicative task before Expanding Your Fluency. For this reason, the order of strands may vary from unit to unit.

Learners are encouraged to perform **Speaking** tasks in pairs and groups. Where appropriate, **strategies** are provided to ensure students' successful communication.

The **Video** section brings the world into the classroom with authentic clips, including news stories, PSAs, and National Geographic documentaries.

Pronunciation boxes offer support and tips as well as cross reference to full explanation and practice in the appendix.

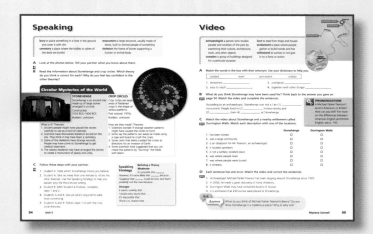

Learners navigate **interesting and relevant readings** from National Geographic through pre-, while-, and post-reading activities, helping them to comprehend the main idea and key details of the passage.

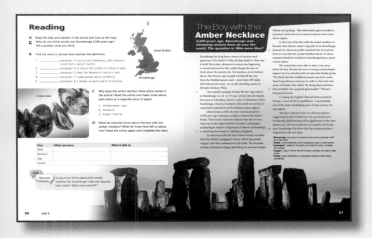

The **Writing** section includes writing models to prompt learners to complete a functional piece of writing and also serves as a culminating activity in many units.

The **Expanding Your Fluency** section allows learners to apply the language they have learned throughout the unit in real-world tasks and offers self-assessment checks.

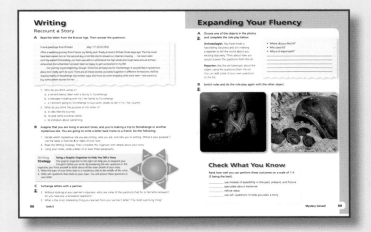

1 Language and Life

1 What kind of communicator are you?

2 In what situations is it hard for you to speak English? When is it not a problem?

3 What is the role of English in the world? What is its effect on other languages?

Unit Outcomes

In this unit, you will learn to:

- use quantifiers to talk about amounts

- bring up negative and sensitive topics

- work with restatement questions

- interpret and question the results of a report

Vocabulary

adapt to change ideas or behavior in order to deal with something successfully

clarify to explain something in order to make it easier to understand

collaborative done by two or more people working together

conflict a serious argument about something important

impulsive doing and saying things suddenly without thinking about it carefully

knowledge information and understanding about a subject

possess to have or to own

remark something that you say (fact or opinion)

sensitive showing an understanding of others' feelings

switch to change

whine to complain in an annoying way about something unimportant

A How do you communicate? Read these questions and think about your answers.

1. Your boss just asked you to lead a very important meeting tomorrow. Do you feel . . .
   a. great? (You love a challenge.)   b. nervous? (You'll be awake all night worrying.)
   c. annoyed? (You are a confident communicator, but don't like being asked at the last minute.)

2. Among your friends, you're the one who . . .
   a. remains calm during conflicts.   b. helps everyone with sensitive issues.
   c. avoids talking about anything uncomfortable.

3. You're having a bad day. Your friend calls to whine about homework. Do you . . .
   a. listen patiently?   b. end the phone call quickly?
   c. switch the topic to your own terrible day?

4. Your idea of a good communicator is someone who . . .
   a. isn't afraid to speak up.   b. can adapt to different conversational topics easily.
   c. possesses a lot of knowledge about many topics.

5. At your friend's wedding, someone passes you the microphone suddenly and asks you to make some congratulatory remarks. You haven't prepared anything to say. Do you . . .
   a. smile and try your best?   b. pass the microphone on to someone else?
   c. pull another friend in to talk with you?

6. You're having a conversation in English when you don't understand what one person has said. Do you . . .
   a. ask the person to clarify?   b. stay silent now and ask for an explanation later?
   c. keep it to yourself and try to figure it out later?

B In pairs, ask each other the questions above. Explain your answers.

C Use two or three of these words to tell your partner what kind of communicator he/she is. Explain why you think so. Does your partner agree?

careful	collaborative	confident	impulsive
nervous	reserved	sensitive	whiney

Grammar

Quantifiers

General amounts	Specific amounts (within a group)
Quantifiers describing general amounts are followed by plural count nouns and noncount nouns.	Quantifiers that describe specific amounts are followed by singular count nouns (except *both* and sometimes *each*).
All students have cell phones.	<u>All members of a group</u>
A lot of students call their parents after school.	**Each/Every student** has a cell phone.
They spend **a lot of time** on their phones.	**Each of **** the **students** has a cell phone.
There are **many students** studying English.	**Any student** in this class can converse in English.
Quite a few students speak English well.	
Some students need help with their homework.	<u>Talking about two things</u>
I have **some free time** and can help you.	The meeting will be on Monday or Tuesday.
A few* students study other foreign languages.	**Both** days** are fine with me.
We don't have **much time** to study for the exam.	**Either day** is fine.
None of the **students** like homework.	**Neither day** works well for me.
*Another common expression with *few* is *very few* (which is an even smaller amount).	****Each of** and **both** are followed by a plural count noun.

large amount ➜

nothing ➜

Much is not used alone in affirmative statements. Use *a lot of* instead: ~~She has much time~~. *She has a lot of time.*

A Read the survey and choose the best answer for each item.

Communication between Teachers and Parents/Students (Percentages refer to "yes" answers.)		Parents	Students
Who works full-time in your family?	fathers	98%	
	mothers	92%	
Do you use our school's Web site to get information?		50%	100%
How do you prefer to get information from teachers?	face-to-face	33%	10%
	e-mail	67%	90%
	telephone	0%	0%

In (1) **many / much** families, (2) **both / neither** parents have full-time jobs. (3) **Some / All** of the students use their school's Web site for information while only (4) **some / all** of the parents do. (5) **A lot of / Very few** students would like to get information from their teachers face-to-face, but (6) **quite a few / very few** parents would. (7) **Both / Either** parents and students prefer to communicate with the teacher by e-mail. (8) **Neither / Either** prefers to get information by telephone. Parents don't have (9) **much / many** time to meet teachers face-to-face at school. Teachers should communicate with parents through (10) **both / neither** e-mail and face-to-face conversations.

B Ask at least three classmates the questions in the survey. Report your results back to a partner.

Listening

> **convey** to express a thought or feeling so that it is understood

A Read the Listening Strategy. Then listen to three statements from a lecture. What is the meaning of the words below? On a separate piece of paper, write your answers. Look at the Listening Strategy again. Which method does the speaker use to define each word in the lecture?

1. content (of your message)
2. objective
3. straightforward

Listening Strategy

Listening for definitions If you are listening to a lecture or a speech, the speaker will often give cues when they are going to define unfamiliar language. Being familiar with these techniques will help you take advantage of these clarifications.

a. Pausing to give the definition within the sentence: *What is the best way to convey—or express—your message clearly?*
b. Using language to signal a definition: *Another way of saying this is: What is the best way to express your ideas clearly?*
c. Asking the audience directly if they know the word: *Do you know what the word* convey *means? It means "to express."*

B Listen to the first part of the lecture and complete the notes.

You	Create a clear message	Choose the right channel
(1) _____ your objective (why?) Know your (2) _____ (who?) Plan the content (what?)	Use this method (K.I.S.S.): **K** (3) _____ **I**t **S**traightforward and **S** (4) _____	What does the person receiving the message (5) _____? How much (6) _____ do you have? Do you need to (7) _____ and (8) _____ a lot of questions? Is the content (9) _____?

PRONUNCIATION As you listen, notice how the speaker stresses certain words in the lecture. Which words do you notice being stressed? For more on stress with content and function words, see p. 144.

C Listen to the second part of the lecture and match the style of communication (a–d) with the person the speaker uses it with. List key words explaining why she uses that style with each person.

a. cell phone
b. text message
c. landline phone[1]
d. video chat

___ 1. husband   reason: _____
___ 2. son   reason: _____
___ 3. mother   reason: _____
___ 4. friend   reason: _____

[1] traditional or home phone

Ask **Answer** Tell your partner one piece of information from the lecture that you found useful. How do you like to communicate with your teacher? Your parents? Your best friend?

Connections

A Would you ever get involved in these situations? Discuss with a partner and explain your answers.

1. Ask a teacher how he / she decided your grade.
2. Critique a coworker's work habits with him / her.
3. Complain to a friend about his / her bad habit.

B Follow the steps below. Be sure to use the vocabulary and grammar from this unit.

1. Read through the three role-play situations and make sure you understand them.
2. Study the language in the box.
3. Choose a role-play with a partner. Use the boxed language to get started.
4. After you finish your role-play, pick another situation and switch roles.

Role-play 1: You and your teacher

Your English essay was due last week. You started on the assignment early, did a lot of research, and worked really hard on it. You just got your paper back from your teacher, and you received a poor grade. You're surprised and frustrated. On top of that, your friend completed the same assignment, wrote half as many pages, and spent almost no time on it. He received a good grade. You want an explanation from your teacher.

Role-play 2: You and your coworker

You are working on an important project at work with one other coworker. You have noticed that your coworker takes long work breaks, and when he's at his desk, he spends a lot of time surfing the Net and chatting with friends on the telephone. You're getting worried that you won't be able to meet your deadline if he doesn't start working harder. You need to talk to him and find out what's going on.

Role-play 3: You and a friend

You're getting frustrated. The last time you met to go to the movies, your friend was thirty-five minutes late. Her tardiness is becoming a habit: She's usually at least thirty minutes late whenever you get together. You know that your friend is very busy being a full-time student and working part-time, but you are tired of waiting for her all the time. You want to talk to her about it.

Bringing up a sensitive topic	Bringing up a negative subject
Can I talk to you for a minute?	I don't mean to be rude, but . . .
Do you mind if I ask you something?	I'm afraid I have some bad news.
I have to tell you something.	I don't know how to tell you this, but . . .
There's something I need to tell you.	

Ask
Answer   Which situation do you think would be the hardest to deal with in real life?

Reading

distinct noticeably separate or different
linguist a person who specializes in the study of languages
preservation protection (for the future)
vanish to disappear

A student in India writes an essay about her school in Punjabi.

A Read the title and subtitle and skim the rest of the article on page 7. On a separate piece of paper, write a short answer to the questions. Read the article to check your answers and make any necessary changes.

  1. Why do you think so many languages are dying out?
  2. What happens when a language dies?

Reading Strategy	**Working with restatement questions** You will see restatement questions like the ones in Exercise **B** on tests. When choosing the best answer, make sure the restatement . . . 1. does not leave out any essential information. 2. does not change the meaning of the original sentence in any significant way.

B Study the Reading Strategy. Then read each sentence (❶, ❷, ❸) in the article on page 7 and choose the best restatement (a, b, or c) for each sentence. Why are the other choices incorrect? Discuss your answers with a partner.

❶ (line 21)   a. It's truly incredible how rich India's linguistic tradition is.
    b. There are many languages in India that we know nothing about.
    c. You can study languages at a basic level and not be able to communicate well.

❷ (line 33)   a. Our values and how we live are different from culture to culture.
    b. When a culture's language disappears, we lose a view of life that we all share.
    c. The main thing that disappears with a language is that culture's distinct view on the human experience.

❸ (line 46)   a. It costs more money to preserve India's culture than it does to protect its languages.
    b. People are already preserving some parts of India's culture and they should also protect its languages.
    c. In a culture that is as rich as India's, we must continue to preserve buildings and animal life.

C With a partner, find words that have the same or similar meanings.

paragraph 1   in danger _____
paragraph 2   release _____
paragraph 5   complicated _____
paragraph 8   old _____

Ask

Answer What minority languages do you know of? Are there any minority languages in your country? What is their status?

What Happens When
a Language Dies?

Experts believe that more than half of the world's roughly seven thousand languages will vanish by the end of this century alone, at the rate of one language every two weeks.

1　India is known for its linguistic and cultural diversity. According to official estimates, the country is home to at least four hundred distinct languages, but many experts believe the actual number is probably around seven hundred. Unfortunately, in a situation that is found in many other countries around the world, many of India's languages are at risk of dying out.

　　The effects of so many languages disappearing could be a cultural disaster. Each language is like a
10　unique key that can unlock local knowledge and attitudes about medicine, the environment, weather and climate patterns, spiritual beliefs, art, and history.

　　A group of linguists working on disappearing languages has identified "hotspots" where local languages are at risk of disappearing. These are places with rich linguistic diversity, but high risk of language extinction because there are few remaining speakers. And in these areas, there is often a lack of recordings or texts that would help with language
20　preservation.

❶ "India has this incredible wealth of languages, but many have not even been described at a basic level," said David Harrison, a linguistics professor at Swarthmore College in the United States.

　　All through history, languages have naturally ebbed and flowed,[1] becoming popular before gradually falling from use. But a complex mix of economic, social, and cultural factors[2] is now causing them to disappear at a faster pace. For example, in rural Indian villages, Hindi or
30　English are popular with younger workers because those languages are often required when they travel to larger towns for work.

❷ "When a language dies, what is primarily lost is the expression of a unique vision of what it means to be human," said David Crystal, honorary professor of linguistics at the University of Wales in the United Kingdom, and author of the book *Language Death*.

　　With growing interest in language diversity, it may be possible for disappearing languages to find new
40　life. Awareness of language preservation has grown due to state-funded language programs and new academic centers created for the study of endangered languages. It's also becoming increasingly possible to study minor languages at the college level, thus helping to ensure[3] their survival.

❸ "Just as people are doing so much to save the tiger or preserve ancient temples in India, it is as important to protect linguistic diversity, which is a part of India's cultural wealth and a monument to human
50　genius," says David Harrison.

[1] ebbed and flowed come and go
[2] factors something that affects an event, decision, or situation
[3] to ensure to guarantee

Video

detect to find or discover that something is present
document to record the details of an event
endure to continue to exist

slave someone who is the property of another person
threatened endangered

A The title of the video you are going to watch is *A Hidden Language Recorded*. What do you think the video is going to be about? Write your answer on a separate piece of paper. Then watch the video and check your answer.

B Read questions 1–4. Then watch the video again and choose the best answer for each question.

1. Why was it difficult for the team to reach their destination?
   a. They didn't have a special permit.
   b. The area was very remote.
   c. They didn't have enough money.

2. Why is Koro a "surprise" language?
   a. because it was unknown previously
   b. because it contains only about eight hundred words
   c. because it's currently spoken only by people under 20

3. What will happen if Koro speakers switch to another language?
   a. They will have better job opportunities.
   b. Their cultural heritage will disappear.
   c. They will be able to communicate more easily.

4. Why did the expedition record Koro speakers?
   a. They wanted to compare it to the other languages.
   b. They wanted to learn to speak it.
   c. They wanted to document it.

C Summarize what you learned from the video. Make some notes and make sure you cover the points below. Then share your summary with a partner.

1. Country where Koro is spoken
2. Number of Koro speakers
3. Possible origin of the language
4. How researchers discovered it
5. Why they want to record it

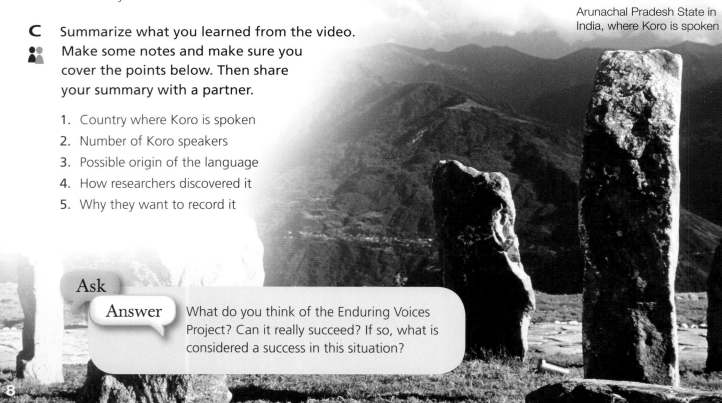

Arunachal Pradesh State in India, where Koro is spoken

Ask

Answer What do you think of the Enduring Voices Project? Can it really succeed? If so, what is considered a success in this situation?

Writing
Write a Report Summary

A Read the summary of a report about English in Europe. Then discuss the questions below with a partner.

Overview

Worldwide, English is the preferred language of the business elite. However, statistics show that the use of English in business, finance, and technology is moving beyond CEOs and upper-level managers to general workers too. Nowadays, not knowing English can affect hiring and advancement opportunities. In Europe, being able to communicate in English is not an option anymore—it's becoming a requirement.

Relevant Information

* Workers who speak English tend to make more money.
* Very few of those who don't speak English are promoted to managerial positions.
* In the Netherlands and Sweden, all students study English from an early age.
* A majority of Europeans surveyed between the ages of 15 and 24 speak English. The number was much smaller for those 55 and older.
* In another survey, almost half of Europeans said they spoke English. Almost a third said they "spoke it well."

Next Steps

* Some countries are behind others in English education. Countries with fewer English speakers must be given financial assistance to increase educational opportunities there.
* Non-English-speaking employees should be offered either on-site English classes or financial support to take classes on their own.
* In many countries, the very young and the very old have fewer opportunities to study English. Special classes must be developed for these sectors of the population.

1. What is the purpose of the report? Why do you think it was created? By whom?
2. Who might read it? Where might you read a report like this?
3. Did any of the information surprise you? Why or why not?
4. What do you think of the suggested next steps? Do you agree with them? Why or why not?

Did you know?

English is considered by some to be a "killer language." As English is given more attention and importance in countries worldwide, speakers of English can "crowd out" or "kill off" the culture and languages of people who speak other languages. In Europe, many minority languages enjoy popularity and government protection, but that is certainly not the case for minority languages internationally.

B Think about the status of English education in your country. Complete the survey with a partner. If you live in a country with minority languages, you may also want to reflect on the status of English versus those languages.

English facts about _____ (country name)

1. **Most / Some / Very few** businesses require employees to speak some English.

   Industries that use English most: _____

2. **Most / Some / Very few** employees who speak English make more money.

3. **All / Some / Very few** children begin studying English in primary school.

4. **All / Some / Very few** people 55 and older speak English.

5. Overall, **all / some / very few** people speak basic English (greetings and simple sentences).

Based on these findings, we would suggest the following:

1. _____

2. _____

3. _____

C Read the Writing Strategy. Then use the information in Exercise **B** to write a report summary together. Use Exercise **A** as a model.

D Join another pair. Read their report summary and answer questions 1–3 in the Writing Checklist.

Writing Checklist

Does the report summary . . .

1. have a brief, clear Overview?

2. use Relevant Information that's easy to understand?

3. give you a clear idea of the Next Steps?

Writing Strategy

Writing a Report Summary

1. Your Overview should give some background and clearly explain the purpose of the report.

2. Choose Relevant Information that best explains the situation simply and clearly. Imagine that someone who has never been to your country is reading this report.

3. For each recommendation in the Next Steps, state the problem in the first sentence. In the second sentence, write your recommendation.

Speaking

A You are going to present your report summary. Decide who will present what. Practice giving your report with a partner.

Speaking Strategy

Interpreting the Results (for the speakers)

The way I see it . . .
As far as I'm concerned . . .
I strongly believe that . . .
Without a doubt, . . .

Questioning the Results (for the listeners)

While ___ may be true, it's also important to remember that . . .
I see your point, but one problem with what you're saying is . . .

B Join another pair and give your report.

1. **Speakers:** Present the report. Interpret what we can learn from the statistics you found. Remember to speak clearly and look at your audience.

2. **Listeners:** After the presentation, if there is anything you disagreed with, speak up.

TIP Practice "reading and looking up." Read a phrase or sentence from your report silently before you speak. Then look up from the text at your audience and say it aloud. This will help you to maintain a connection with your audience.

Expanding Your Fluency

Loanwords in English are words that are taken from another language, sometimes with a change in meaning. An example of a loanword from Spanish to English is *aficionado*, which means "fan" in both languages.

A Read through the questions with a partner. Make sure you understand them.

1. This word, which describes **a yellow-skinned fruit loved by monkeys**, came to English from Africa through Spanish or Portuguese. What is the English word?	2. The **samovar** is a metal container used to heat water for tea. Samovars became widely popular in the city of St. Petersburg in the nineteenth century. What country is the word **samovar** from?	3. This word refers to **a permanent mark or design made on the skin with ink.** In the Tahitian language, you say "tatu." What is the word in English?	4. In Swedish, the word "isberg" means "ice mountain." In English, the loanword means **"a huge piece of ice floating in the ocean."** What is the word in English?
5. This popular morning beverage comes from the Arabic word "qahwah" and **it may be named after the Kaffa region** in Ethiopia. What is the word for this drink in English?	6. You might want some of this **red sauce** (from the Chinese word "koechiap") the next time you have a hamburger. What is the word in English?	7. The word "broccoli" in English comes from **a European country that is known for its appreciation of good food and wine.** What is the name of that country?	8. In Persian, the word "paejamah" can be divided into "pae" (leg) and "jamah" (clothing). In English, the word refers to **something you would put on before bedtime.** What is the word in English?

B Join another pair. Take turns asking each other the questions. Score one point for each correct answer.

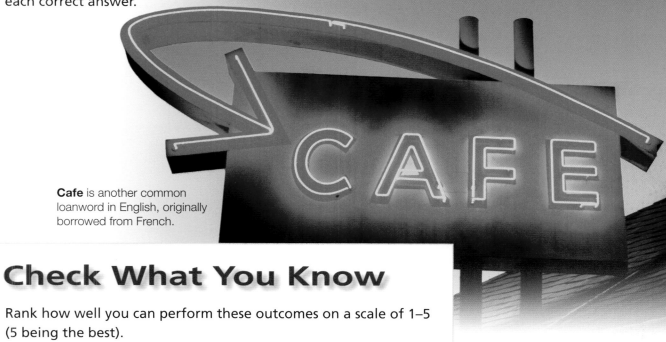

Cafe is another common loanword in English, originally borrowed from French.

Check What You Know

Rank how well you can perform these outcomes on a scale of 1–5 (5 being the best).

_____ use quantifiers to talk about amounts

_____ bring up negative and sensitive topics

_____ work with restatement questions

_____ interpret and question the results of a report

2 Money Talks

1 Read the title of the unit. If money could talk, what do you think it would say?

2 Look at the photo. Where do you think this place is? What do you think the people are doing? What is the bowl on the ground for?

3 In general, would you say that you are good or bad with money? Explain.

Unit Outcomes

In this unit, you will learn to:

- describe spending habits and preferences

- use noun clauses to explain thoughts in more detail

- determine the meaning of unfamiliar words in a text

- consider the advantages and disadvantages of something

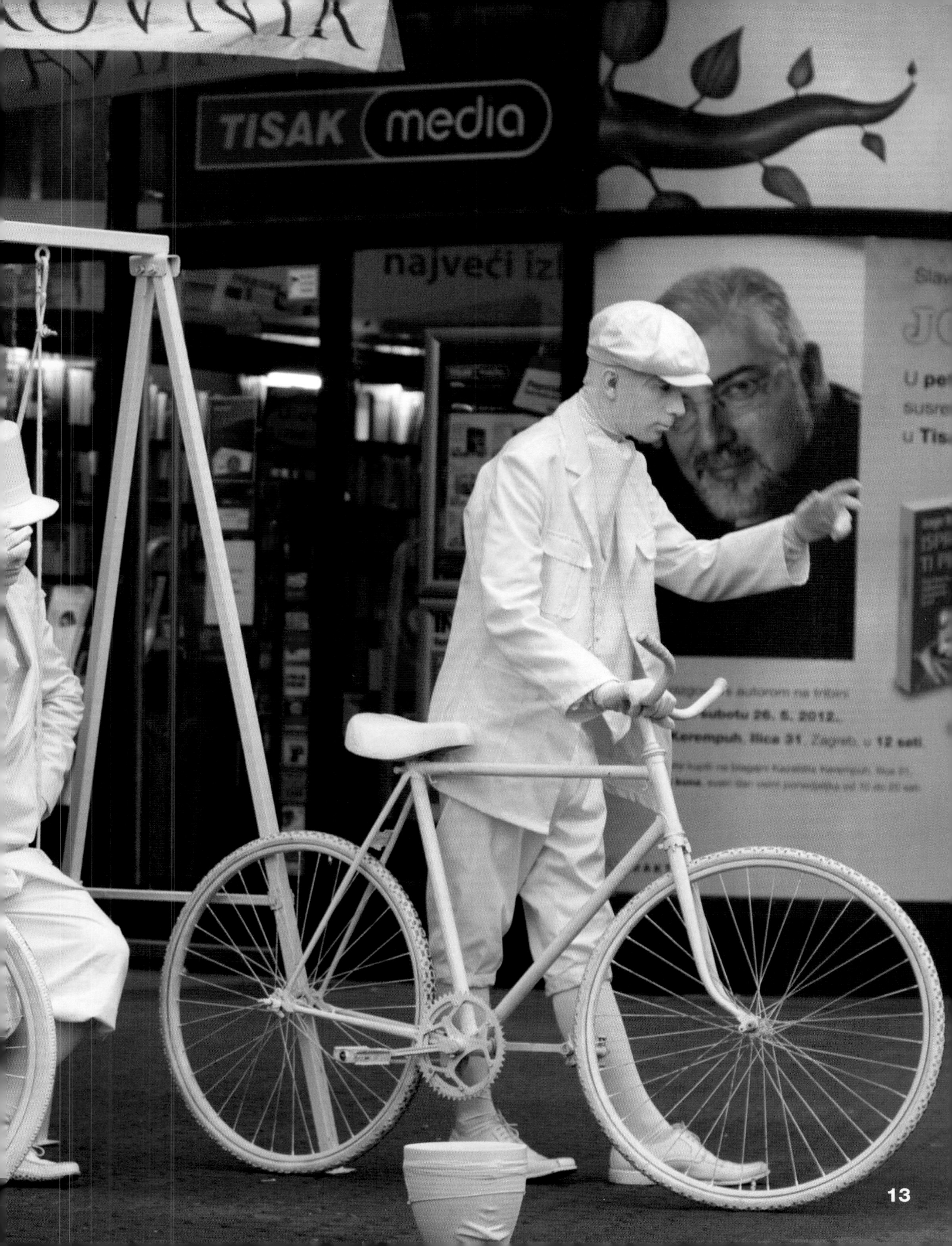
TISAK media

Vocabulary

affluent wealthy

budget a plan that shows the amount of money available to spend

credit a method that allows you to buy things and pay for them later

debt money that you owe

disposable income the money remaining after your bills are paid

loan money you borrow or lend

materialistic valuing money and possessions very highly

pay back to return money that you owe someone

sacrifice to give up something valuable to help yourself or others

save up (for something) to put aside money for future use

splurge to spend a lot of money on something, usually something you don't need

thrifty careful with money

value to attach importance to something

Word Partnership

What do these expressions that use *credit* mean?
~ card, ~ history, live on ~, good/bad ~

A Read the two profiles. Try to guess which word from the word bank completes each sentence. Then listen and write the correct form of the word.

Lukas

My parents took loans and went into (1) _____ to buy a house and lots of expensive things. They lived on credit, and today they're still (2) _____ the money they owe. I, on the other hand, have always stayed within a budget. I rent a small but comfortable apartment, ride my bike places, and spend less overall. I guess we just (3) _____ different things.

Carla

My parents worked hard and saved up to send me to a good university. They (4) _____ a lot for me and always worried about money. Today, I'm a successful businesswoman with a disposable income that my parents never had. I've got a beautiful home, take regular vacations, and (5) _____ on nice things for myself once in a while— and why shouldn't I?

B Discuss the questions with a partner.

1. Which words from the word bank describe Lukas and Carla? How about their parents? Why?
2. How have things changed for each of these people in one generation?
3. Can you relate to any of these people's experiences? Explain with an example.

C Think of two more questions. Each should use a different item from the word bank. Then take turns asking and answering the questions with a partner.

1. What's something you're saving up for?
2. Are you a thrifty person?
3. _____?
4. _____?

Grammar

Noun Clauses

noun clauses starting with *that*	I like this jacket. How much is it?
	I think **(that) it is $50**.
noun clauses starting with a *wh-* word	I like this jacket. How much is it?
	I don't know **how much it is**.

Some **noun clauses** begin with the word *that*.
Other **noun clauses** begin with a *wh-* word (*who, what, where, why, how, when, which, whose*). These clauses follow statement word order even though they start with a question word.

Certain verbs are commonly followed by a noun clause . . .
- verbs that describe an opinion, feeling, or mental state: *assume, believe, guess, forget, hope, know, remember, suppose, think, understand, wonder*
- verbs that describe something someone said: *admit, explain, mention, say, tell*

A Choose the correct answer for each sentence. Then check answers and practice the dialog with a partner.

A: Joe eats out every day. I wonder how (1) **can he / he can** afford it.

B: He (2) **told me / told to me that** he just got a new job.

A: Do you know (3) **where is he / where he is** working?

B: I think (4) **that is at / he works at** a cafe near school.

B Change the question to a noun clause that starts with a *wh-* word.

1. I've just inherited some money. What should I do with it?
   I don't know <u>what I should do with it</u>.

2. Nadia's brother is jealous because she earns more money than he does. Why does he feel that way?
   I wonder _____ .

3. Some people love to shop. Why do they like it?
   I don't get _____ .

4. I need to get some money. Where's the closest ATM?
   Do you know _____?

5. I owe a lot on my credit card. How can I pay the money back fast?
   Can you suggest _____?

6. I missed class yesterday. What did we do?
   Do you remember _____?

C With a partner, create short dialogs using the situations in Exercise **B**. In each dialog try to use at least one noun clause starting with *that*.

I've just inherited some money, but I don't know what I should do with it.

I guess that you could splurge on something like a vacation or a new car, but it's probably best to save the money.

Listening

A Look at the photos and then discuss the questions with a partner.

1. How much money do people typically spend on a wedding in your country?
2. Is it worth spending a lot of money on a big TV? Explain your answer.

B You are going to hear two short dialogs. Listen and check the answers that are true about the people. List any key words that helped you make your choices. Then check answers with a partner.

Josh and Tina . . .	True	Key words
1. are planning to get married this year.	☐	_____
2. want to have a large wedding.	☐	_____
3. come from affluent families.	☐	_____

Marta . . .	True	Key words
1. has enough money to buy the big TV.	☐	_____
2. has a budget for how much she can spend on a TV.	☐	_____
3. decides to splurge and get the big TV.	☐	_____

C Play the dialogs again and listen for the words in italics. Then choose the correct answers.

1. *cost a fortune* = Something costs **a lot / very little**.
2. *out of my price range* = Something is **really affordable / too expensive**.
3. *maxed out* = The credit card will have **enough / no** credit left.
4. *a steal* = Something is really **cheap / expensive**.

D Discuss the questions with a partner.

1. In Dialog 1, how does the man feel about Josh and Tina's decision? Why? Would you want a wedding like theirs? Why or why not?
2. In Dialog 2, do you think Marta made the right decision? Why or why not? What is something that is out of your price range that you wish you could buy? Why do you want it?

Connections

A Get into a group of three people and do the following:

1. Read the questions. Then together write two more questions of your own. Each question should be related to the topic of money.

   Would you be willing to . . .

   a. loan money to a good friend who might not be able to pay you back?

   b. marry someone who was poor or in debt?

   c. give up your seat on an airplane for cash (and take a different flight the next day)?

   d. use a credit card to splurge on something really expensive?

   e. _____?

   f. _____?

2. On your own, think about your answers to each question.

3. Take six small pieces of paper. Write the letters *a* to *f* on each. Shuffle the papers and place them face down in a pile.

4. One person starts. Turn over a paper and answer that question. (You should not answer the same question twice.) Use one of the expressions in the strategy box to get started. Then explain your answer. Try to speak for at least one minute. Your group members should each ask you one question.

5. When you are done, return the paper to the bottom of the pile. Then it is the next person's turn.

6. Play until everyone has answered all of the questions.

> **Speaking Strategy**
>
> **Expressing an Opinion**
> Yeah, definitely because . . .
> I think so . . .
> I guess/suppose so, but . . .
> I don't know what I'd do, but I guess . . .
> I don't think so . . ./I doubt it.
> No way./Definitely not.

> **Notice!** Some noun clauses can be shortened using *so*.
> Would you loan money to a friend?
> **I (don't) think so.** = I (don't) think that I'd loan money to him.

Reading

A Complete sentences 1 and 2 with words from the box and check answers with a partner. Then look at the photo. This person needs to borrow money to pay for university. Do you think a bank will lend her money? Why or why not?

collateral	interest	lend	qualify

1. To _____ for a bank loan, you must have good credit and even some _____ (extra money, a house or car that you already own). If you don't have these things, a bank won't _____ you the money.

2. When you borrow money from a bank, you have to pay a fee called _____ on the money you borrowed.

B Read the strategy box and then the entire article on the next page. When you are done, write a simple definition or synonym for the five boldfaced words on a separate piece of paper. Try to work out the meaning on your own. Then check answers with a partner.

Age: 21
Occupation: Part-time cashier in store
Credit history: $300 in the bank, one credit card with $600 on it, doesn't own a car or any property

> **Reading Strategy**
>
> **Determine the Meaning of Unfamiliar Words in a Text**
> 1. Sometimes it is possible to understand the meaning of unfamiliar words in a reading by analyzing the word's parts: *il* (meaning *not*) + *legible* (meaning *readable*) = difficult to read.
> 2. You can also use surrounding words to help you: *It's a new type of banking called micro-credit, which gives small loans to poor people.*

C Re-read paragraphs 1 and 2 and then answer the questions on a separate piece of paper.

1. What is micro-credit banking?
2. How is micro-credit banking different from traditional bank loans? List two examples.
3. What is the relationship of each of these numbers to Muhammad Yunus and micro-credit banking?

1976	$5.7 billion	96%	a few hundred US dollars	98%

D How does Kiva work? Complete steps 1–7 and then explain the process to a partner.

1. A person who wants to borrow money visits _____.
2. The person is interviewed to make sure _____.
3. The borrower's profile is then _____.
4. People around the world can then read that profile, _____, and _____.
5. The borrower uses the money to _____.
6. The borrower then has a certain amount of time to _____.
7. Finally, the money is _____ the lender's account.

> **Ask**
> **Answer** Do you think that micro-lending has been successful? Explain with specific examples from the article.

MICRO LOANS, MACRO IMPACT

Muhammad Yunus

1   They call Muhammad Yunus the "banker of the poor." The economist[1] from Bangladesh and his Grameen Bank **pioneered** a new type of banking known as micro-credit. This type of banking gives small loans to poor people who have no collateral and who do not qualify for traditional bank loans. The program, which Yunus founded in 1976, has enabled millions of Bangladeshis to buy everything from cows to cell phones in order to start and run their own businesses. Since then, Grameen Bank
10   has made an estimated $5.7 billion in loans to more than six million people in Bangladesh, 96% of them women.

Anyone can qualify for the loans, which average a few hundred US dollars. No collateral or credit history is necessary, nor is completing a lot of paperwork (as many of those applying for the loans are **illiterate**). A borrower can only apply for future loans after repaying some of his or her current debts, and to date, the system has a repayment rate of 98%, the bank says. "A hundred dollars may be all a poor person needs to get out of poverty,"
20   says Alex Counts, who worked with Yunus in Bangladesh for six years. "You give them a fair deal[2] . . . and they're able to put their motivation and skills to work."

Today, micro-credit projects like Yunus' are helping many around the world. One is an Internet-based lending company called Kiva. It was started in 2005 by two Stanford University graduates who attended a talk given by Muhammad Yunus. Kiva works by connecting regular people who have some extra money to lend with entrepreneurs[3] who need it.

30   How does the process work? A person who wants to borrow money first visits one of Kiva's "field partners." (These are micro-lending institutions in countries all over the world.) The person is interviewed to make sure that he or she is **legitimate** and will be using the loan in a legal way. Then the person's profile is posted on the Kiva Web site. People around the world can read that profile, open an account on the Kiva site, and make a loan. The person who borrowed the money might use it to start a business, attend school, open a clinic, or build
40   housing. The borrower then has a certain amount of time to repay the money, which is eventually **deposited** back into the lender's account. Lenders receive no interest, though most field partners working with Kiva charge the borrower a fee. Some fees are as little as 8% of the original loan, while others are higher. According to Kiva, more than 700,000 people have received loans, and over 98% of those people have paid back the money.

Yunus, who won the Nobel Peace Prize for his work, believes that offering people micro-loans not
50   only helps them to get out of poverty; it also promotes peace and stability.[4] Sam Daley-Harris, who worked

> ## " A hundred dollars may be all a poor person needs to get out of poverty."

with Yunus, agrees. Achieving peace is about more than stopping war, he says. "A key part of **preventing** conflict is enabling people . . . to care for themselves and their children." This is what micro-credit programs like Grameen Bank and Kiva are helping people to do.

[1] **economist** a person who studies the way in which money is used in society
[2] **fair deal** a good business arrangement
[3] **entrepreneur** a person who starts his or her own business
[4] **stability** a situation that is calm and not likely to change suddenly

Video

---

headache a big problem

impact to have an effect on someone or something

run out (of something) to have no more of something

snowball to increase rapidly

terms the parts of the contract that all sides must agree on (e.g., how much a loan is for, how long one has to pay it back, etc.)

A Think about what you've already learned from the article about borrowing and lending money. Then discuss the questions with a partner.

1. Why would a person borrow money from a bank?
2. What are some of the benefits of being able to borrow money from a bank? What are some of the risks?

B Watch segment 1 of the video. Then choose the best answer to complete the sentences.

1. You might watch this video to learn . . . .

   a. which banks are the best to borrow from
   b. about the history of banking in the United States
   c. how borrowing money from a bank works

2. The *interest rate* on a loan is . . . .

   a. a fine you pay for not repaying the bank
   b. the money you borrow from the bank
   c. a fee you pay for borrowing money

C Rachel is a musician who needs to borrow some money. Read the outline. Then watch segment 2 of the video and complete the outline.

Recording an album

A. Reason she needs to borrow money: _____

   How much she needs: $_____

B. First loan terms:

   • _____% APR (annual percentage rate)
   • Must pay back the loan in _____ year(s)
   • Payment amount per month: $_____
   • If she accepted this loan, she would _____ of money in _____ months.

C. She finally finds a loan with a _____ APR and a _____ time frame.

D Before accepting her loan, what two important things did Rachel learn? Watch segment 3 and choose your answers. Then tell a partner why knowing those two things is important.

☐ the importance of making payments on time

☐ some banks don't lend money to students

☐ how to budget your money

☐ interest rates can change

E Discuss the questions with a partner.

1. Why was Rachel able to pay back her loan on time?
2. In recent years, some banks have allowed people to take loans that were difficult—sometimes even impossible—to pay back. Why would a bank do this? Why is doing this a problem for both the borrower and the bank?

Speaking

> **profit** money that is earned in business minus expenses

A Get into a group of six people: three will be borrowers (entrepreneurs); the other three will be lenders (investors).

INVESTORS: You're all billionaire investors looking for "the next big thing." You give money to entrepreneurs with great ideas in return for a percentage of the profits they eventually earn.

You're going to interview three entrepreneurs. Each one thinks he/she has a great idea, but they all need a large amount of money to get started. You only want to invest in ideas that are likely to make you money.

Read the three questions in the entrepreneurs' section and together think of others you could ask.

ENTREPRENEURS: You need a large amount of money to do something important. On your own . . .

1. Select a reason or think of your own idea.
   - To start a business or invent a product
   - To record an album or film a movie
   - To open a school
   - To build housing
   - Your idea: _____

2. Answer the questions on a separate piece of paper. You can invent information or use real facts. You have to impress the investors, so be creative.
   - What do you plan to do with the money?
   - Why do you think your idea will be a big success and make you and the investors a lot of money?
   - How much money do you need to get started?

Grand opening

B Each investor should pair up with an entrepreneur. The investor should use his or her questions to interview the entrepreneur and take notes on the person's replies. Repeat this step until each investor has interviewed each entrepreneur. You will have three minutes per interview.

C When the interviews are over, do the following:

- **Investors:** On your own, review your notes. Of the three entrepreneurs you interviewed, who do you want to invest in—all of them, one of them, or none of them? Why?
- **Entrepreneurs:** Get together in a group of three. Explain to the other entrepreneurs what you need money to do. Do you think you're going to get it? Why or why not?

D Get back together in your original group from Exercise **A**. Each investor should take turns explaining their investment decision to the group. Were the investors' choices the same? Which entrepreneur's idea was the most popular?

E Change roles and repeat Exercises **A** through **D**.

Writing
Write about Advantages and Disadvantages

A What are some of the advantages and disadvantages of using a credit card? With a partner, list as many
ideas as you can on a separate piece of paper. Then compare ideas with the class.

B Read the paragraphs and then answer the questions below.

> Using a credit card has advantages and disadvantages. **One obvious advantage is that** you can buy anything you want or need immediately, even if it is expensive. Let's say, for example, that you really need a new laptop, but you don't have the money for it. Instead of waiting and saving up for it, you could use your credit card to buy the computer and pay for it a little at a time. **Another benefit of using a credit card is that** you can earn points on some cards to buy things. Each time you buy something with your card, you get points. Later you can use these to get other things for free.
>
> There are disadvantages of using credits cards, though. **One disadvantage is that** a credit card makes it too easy to buy things. If you go into a store and have $50, for example, you can only spend that much money. But with a credit card, you can buy many more things, including things you can't afford. This can cause you to go into debt. **Another drawback is that** . . .

Start the essay with a clear topic sentence that tells your readers what the text is about

Use the boldfaced phrases to introduce and transition from one idea to the next.

1. What two advantages does the writer mention in the first paragraph?
2. The writer explains each advantage with an example. Underline each example in the paragraph.
3. What is another disadvantage of having a credit card? Finish the second paragraph with your own idea. Remember to include an example to explain your point. Then compare ideas with a partner.

C Complete steps 1 and 2 below.

1. Many students today must get a loan to attend university. What are the advantages and disadvantages of taking a large loan to attend university? Outline two advantages and two disadvantages on a separate piece of paper. Think of an example to support each one.

2. Use your outline to write a two-paragraph essay. Remember to start off with a clear topic sentence, explain each advantage and disadvantage with a detailed example, and use the boldfaced phrases from Exercise **B** to transition from one idea to the next.

D Exchange papers with a partner. Read your partner's essay and use the checklist to make sure the
essay is complete.

Writing Checklist

The essay . . .

- has a clear topic sentence.
- identifies two advantages and two disadvantages and explains each with a detailed example.
- uses the boldfaced phrases in Exercise **B** to introduce and transition from one idea to the next.

Expanding Your Fluency

👥 **Read the six situations (a–f) below. Then do steps 1–3 with a partner.**

1. Write a simple definition for each underlined word or phrase.
2. Identify if each underlined word or phrase is related to saving or spending money.
3. Use at least one of the underlined words or phrases and other vocabulary you learned in this unit to write a short dialog. Then perform your dialog for another pair.

   a. I've got a <u>nest egg</u> of $100,000 in my bank account that I can use as a down payment on a condo.
   b. Lunch is <u>my treat</u> today. You paid for it the last time we went out together.
   c. Martin is more than thrifty; he's a total <u>cheapskate</u>. He never spends money on *anything*.
   d. We know the restaurant's owner so our meals were <u>on the house</u>. We didn't pay for anything.
   e. It's hard to <u>make ends meet</u> every month when you don't make a lot of money.
   f. I'm <u>broke</u>. Could you lend me $50 until payday? I promise I'll pay you back.

Check What You Know

Rank how well you can perform these outcomes on a scale of 1–5 (5 being the best).

_____ describe spending habits and preferences
_____ use noun clauses to explain thoughts in more detail
_____ determine the meaning of unfamiliar words in a text
_____ consider the advantages and disadvantages of something

3 Bright Lights, Big Cities

1 What are some of the challenges of living in a big city?

2 What factors make a city a nice place to live?

3 How does the movement of people affect life in the city? Life in the countryside?

Unit Outcomes

In this unit, you will learn to:

- express actions and conditions in the passive voice

- use an outline to summarize

- use statistics to understand a writer's point of view

- write a summary

Vocabulary

chaotic in a state of complete disorder
community a group of people that live in a
 particular place
cosmopolitan full of people from many different
 countries
descendants people of later generations
district an area of a town or country
dynamic full of energy

global affecting all parts of the world; international
immigrant a person who moves permanently to a
 different country
inhabitant a person who lives in a particular place
livable suitable for living in
manageable able to be dealt with easily
metropolitan relating to a large, busy city

A Read these descriptions of different international destinations. Match
each description with the city it describes. (One city is not used.)

a. Cairo, Egypt
b. Moscow, Russia
c. New York, USA

d. São Paulo, Brazil
e. Sydney, Australia

Word Partnership

How many words with
mega- (= extremely large)
and *multi-* (= large number)
can you locate below? What
do they mean?

CITIES OF THE WORLD QUIZ

___ 1. This multiethnic city has major communities composed of the descendants of European, Asian, and African immigrants. In fact, the world's largest Japanese population outside of Japan lives in the Liberdade neighborhood in this city. **Fun thing to do:** Join in the Carnival fun.

___ 2. In the 1930s, this city's population was over ten million, making it the world's first "megacity." A third of the inhabitants of this multicultural city come from other countries and it is the home to many multinational corporations. **Fun thing to do:** Take the ferry to the Statue of Liberty.

___ 3. Home to approximately seventeen million people in its metropolitan area, this megapolis is known as the "Mother of the World." This dynamic and chaotic city is a great home base for sightseeing trips. **Fun thing to do:** Visit the oldest district in the city and see walls from Roman times.

Moscow, one of the
most populous cities
in the world

___ 4. Small enough to be manageable, yet large enough to maintain a cosmopolitan atmosphere, this global city of sea and surf is often rated as one of the most livable cities in the world. **Fun thing to do:** Go sailing under the Harbour Bridge or take a jog along the cliffs.

B Answer the questions with a partner.

1. How many inhabitants are there in the
 metropolitan area nearest you?

2. Which adjective(s) would you use to
 describe this metropolitan area?

3. Does your area have many immigrants?
 Where are they from?

4. Is there a lot of construction and growth
 going on where you live?

5. What's the most interesting district where
 you live? Why?

Grammar

> **Notice!** The form for the dynamic and stative passive is the same: a form of *be* + the past participle.

Dynamic and Stative Passive

Dynamic Passive	Stative Passive
Belize City, the former capital, **was** nearly **destroyed** by a hurricane in 1961. The government **was moved** to Belmopan in 1970.	Belmopan, the new capital, **is situated** inland on safer ground, but Belize City **is** still **known** as the financial and cultural center of the country.
• This form of the passive expresses an action. The focus is on the receiver of the action, not the performer. • Use *by* + agent to name the performer of the action. (We don't use a *by* phrase when the performer is unimportant, unknown, or is obvious.) • The past participle functions more like a verb than an adjective. It expresses the action.	• This form of the passive describes a state or condition. • Because there is no action being expressed, it's impossible to name the agent. • Instead, we use a form of the passive followed by a preposition (not necessarily *by*). • The past participle functions more like an adjective than a verb. It describes the subject.
Verbs used with dynamic passive: built, created, destroyed, divided, moved, sent	*Verbs used with stative passive: acquaint (with), associate (with), cover (with), crowd (with), dress (in), involve (with), know (as), made (of), situate (on)*

A Read about the Nebuta Festival. Complete the description with the passive forms of the verbs in parentheses. Add a preposition when necessary. Which passive forms are stative and which are dynamic?

A FUN THING TO DO IN MY CITY

You may not _____ (1. acquaint) the Nebuta Festival. It _____ (2. organize) the city of Aomori, in northern Japan. The main part of the festival is a nighttime parade. Special colorful floats _____ (3. prepare) people in the community. The frames of these floats _____ (4. make) wood and _____ (5. cover) beautiful paper. The inside of each float _____ (6. illuminate) special lights that make them glow. Then the brightly lit floats _____ (7. carry) city residents through the streets. The streets _____ (8. crowd) spectators as well as festival dancers, who _____ (9. dress) special costumes. The dancers _____ (10. accompany) loud drumming music, and the dancers chant noisily as they move through the streets. If you want to _____ (11. involve) the festival, even as a tourist, you can! You just have to rent a costume to dance! The festival _____ (12. associate) an old legend. It is said that many centuries ago, the colorful floats _____ (13. use) soldiers in battle. The soldiers hid inside them in order to trick their enemies.

B Work with a partner. Think of a major event in a city that you know. Use these questions to make some notes about it, but don't write the name of the event down.

- Is the event well known around the world?
- When and where is the event held?
- Why is it celebrated? Is it associated with a particular person or historical event?
- Will you see people dressed in special clothes?
- Are any special foods prepared on that day?
- When will it be celebrated next?

C Present the notes about your event to another pair without naming it. Can they guess what it is?

Bright Lights, Big Cities

Listening

Word Partnership

urban ~renewal, ~planning, ~community, ~development, ~sprawl

rapid fast

renewal the act of restoring

A Frank and Jane are talking about the city of Curitiba, Brazil. Listen to the first part of their conversation. Then choose the best answer to complete each sentence.

1. Frank is going to Curitiba for **business / pleasure / school**.
2. Jane visited Curitiba for **business / pleasure / school**.

B Now listen to Frank and Jane's entire conversation. Which one of these topics was *not* mentioned?

a famous person   sightseeing tips   weather conditions

cheap flights   transportation system

C Read the outline. Use the topics in Exercise **B** to complete the information. Then listen and complete the rest of the outline.

Curitiba, Brazil

I. _____

    A. best in Brazil

        1. makes the city very _____

    B. constructed in the _____

        1. went from 25,000 to _____ riders a day

II. _____: Jaime Lerner

    A. the _____ for many years

        1. associated with positive changes

        2. devoted to creating a _____ city

        3. reduced city's dependence on _____

        4. supported new _____ transit line

III. _____

    A. the _____ Line comes every 30 minutes

        1. visits major parks and attractions

    B. see _____ influence in architecture, customs, and food

IV. _____

    A. bring a _____ for the cool _____ at night

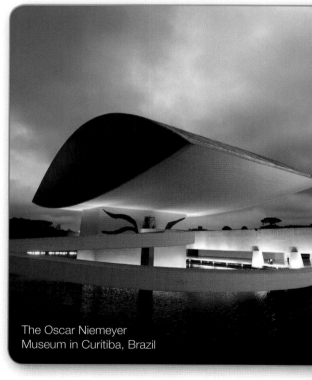

The Oscar Niemeyer Museum in Curitiba, Brazil

D Using your outline in Exercise **C**, summarize for your partner what Curitiba is known for. What is your city known for? Tell your partner two or three ideas.

Connections

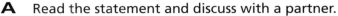

ban to refuse to allow

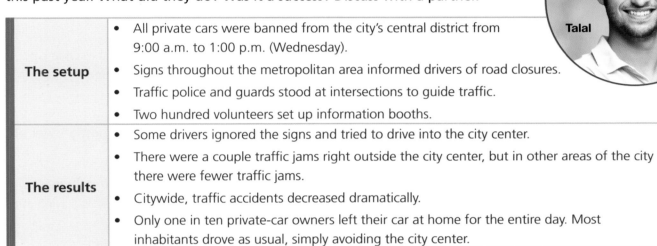

A Read the statement and discuss with a partner.
Do you agree or disagree with it? What kind of small changes could make your city more livable?

Every city can be improved in less than three years by making a series of small changes.

B Talal's city celebrated World Carfree Day (September 22) for the first time this past year. What did they do? Was it a success? Discuss with a partner.

Talal

The setup	• All private cars were banned from the city's central district from 9:00 a.m. to 1:00 p.m. (Wednesday). • Signs throughout the metropolitan area informed drivers of road closures. • Traffic police and guards stood at intersections to guide traffic. • Two hundred volunteers set up information booths.
The results	• Some drivers ignored the signs and tried to drive into the city center. • There were a couple traffic jams right outside the city center, but in other areas of the city there were fewer traffic jams. • Citywide, traffic accidents decreased dramatically. • Only one in ten private-car owners left their car at home for the entire day. Most inhabitants drove as usual, simply avoiding the city center.

C Now work with a partner to plan a World Carfree Day where you live. Read the rules and complete the details. Then discuss the questions together.

RULES:

1. World Carfree Day events should be between four and twelve hours long.
2. The carfree area should be at least 5 square kilometers.

DETAILS:

1. The _____ area / district is located in _____ .
   (name of area)   (city)

2. We will be closing this area / district to _____ from _____ to _____ on _____ .
   (type of transportation)   (start time)   (end time)   (day of the week)

• Some people are not acquainted with World Carfree Day. How do you plan to advertise it?
• The streets just outside the carfree zone will be filled with vehicles. What will you do to handle that situation?
• How will your plans be coordinated with the public transportation system (buses, trains, etc.) where you live?
• How will you prepare drivers for road closures and any other inconveniences?

D Share your idea for World Carfree Day with another pair of students.

Reading

infrastructure the basic facilities (such as transportation, power supplies, and buildings) that allow a city or organization to function

per capita (the amount) per person

transformation a complete change in the appearance of something (usually for the better)

urbanization the process by which more and more people move from rural areas to the cities

A Skim the article on page 31. What is it about? Complete the sentence.

The article is about the _____ rapid urbanization in Seoul, South Korea.

a. history of   b. pros and cons of   c. author's experience of   d. failure of

> **Reading Strategy**
>
> **Locating and Reading Statistics** Locate and read the statistical information (as well as the sentences around it) in an article. Paying attention to the kinds of statistics that the author has chosen to present may tell you about his/her overall point of view (positive, negative, or neutral).

B Read the article and match the numbers to what they describe. Then choose the best answer about the author's point of view.

___ 1. paragraph 1: *fewer than three million to ten million*
___ 2. paragraph 1: *less than one hundred*
___ 3. paragraph 2: *1394*
___ 4. paragraph 3: *more than a million*
___ 5. paragraph 5: *half the people*
___ 6. paragraph 6: *twenty-four million*
___ 7. paragraph 6: *28% to 83%*
___ 8. paragraph 6: *fifty-one years to seventy-nine years*

a. people arriving in Seoul after the wars
b. change in percentage of people living in cities
c. change in Seoul's population
d. change in average life expectancy
e. per capita GDP in dollars (before)
f. Seoul's current population
g. the year Seoul was founded
h. people who have bought their own apartments

The author's overall point of view of Seoul's rapid urbanization is **positive / neutral / negative**.

C What do these phrases/sentences from the article refer to or mean? Discuss with a partner.

1. paragraph 3: *The explosive energy of my generation . . .*
2. paragraph 4: *You can't understand urbanization in isolation from economic development.*
3. paragraph 7: *The chances are close to zero.*

Ask

Answer How have the residents of Seoul benefited from the city's rapid urbanization? Can you think of any disadvantages of such rapid growth? Compare a city near you to Seoul. How are they similar/different?

RAPID URBANIZATION: A Case Study

▶ **There is no single model for how to manage rapid urbanization, but there are hopeful examples. One is Seoul, the capital of South Korea.**

1　Between 1960 and 2000 Seoul's population grew from fewer than three million to ten million. South Korea, once one of the world's poorest countries with a per capita GDP of less than $100, became richer than some countries in Europe. The speed of the transformation shows. Driving into Seoul on the highway along the Han River, you pass an area of large concrete apartment blocks. They may not be very interesting on the outside, but as urban planner Yeong-Hee Jang put it, life inside
10　"is so warm and convenient."

　　Seoul was a "planned city" from the start. The site was chosen as the capital in 1394. Its location, with the Han River to the south and a large mountain to the north, offered good protection from the northern winds. For five centuries it stayed a closed-off city of a few hundred thousand people. Then the twentieth century changed everything.

　　World War II and then the Korean War, which South Korea agreed to stop fighting in 1953, brought more than a million people into Seoul. They wanted to improve
20　their lives. The "explosive energy of my generation," says Hong-Bin Kang, a former vice mayor who now runs Seoul's history museum, dates from this period. So does South Korea's population explosion, which happened due to rapid improvements in public health and nutrition.[1]

　　Over the years, Korean companies grew stronger. Central to the process, which created corporations like Samsung and
30　Hyundai, were the men and women coming into Seoul to work in its new factories and educate themselves at its universities. "You can't understand urbanization in isolation[2] from economic development," says economist Kyung-Hwan Kim of Sogang University. The growing city enabled economic growth, which paid for the infrastructure that helped
40　the city handle the country's growing population.

If you lived in old Seoul, north of the Han River, in the 1970s and 1980s, you watched an entirely new Seoul rise on the south bank, in the area called Kangnam. Over the years an increasing share of the population has been able to make money and live better due to an improving economy. And because the inhabitants of Seoul have been able to make more money, today half of them have been able to buy their own apartments.

50　Today Seoul is one of the densest[3] cities (twenty-four million in the metropolitan area) in the world. It has millions of cars but also an excellent subway system. The streets are busy with commerce and crowded with pedestrians. Life has gotten much better for Koreans as the country has gone from 28% urban in 1961 to 83% today. Life expectancy has increased from 51 years to 79. Korean boys now grow 6 inches (over 15 centimeters) taller than they used to.

　　South Korea's experience can't be easily copied, but it does prove that a poor country can urbanize
60　successfully and incredibly fast. In the late 1990s Kyung-Hwan Kim worked for the UN in Nairobi, advising African cities on their difficult financial problems. "Every time I visited one of these cities I asked myself, What would a visiting expert have said to Koreans in 1960?" he says. "Would he have imagined Korea as it was fifty years later? The chances are close to zero."

[1] **nutrition** the foods that you take into your body (and how they influence your health)
[2] **in isolation (from)** separately (from)
[3] **dense** containing a lot of people or things in a small area; crowded

Urban renewal in Seoul created recreation space around Cheonggyecheon Stream.

Video

> **destruction** the state of being destroyed
> **drought** a long period of time in which no rain falls
> **soil** the substance on the surface of the Earth in which plants grow; dirt
> **stunt** to prevent something from growing as much as it should

A Read this information in preparation for watching the video.
Use your dictionary to look up any unfamiliar words.

Nomads are people who move from place to place rather than living in one place all
the time: In the open **steppe** of northern Mongolia, **herding** nomads **migrate**
in search of food and resources, moving based on **climate** changes.

B The video is about nomads giving up their lives and moving to the
cities. Choose the main cause for these migrations. Then watch
segment 1 and check your prediction.

weather changes on the steppe   better housing in the city
job opportunities in the city   a lack of interest in herding

> A *ger*, a tent used
> by Mongolian
> nomads, outside
> Mongolia's captia

C Watch segment 2 and complete the flow charts.

1. _____ change → partly drives _____
2. hard _____ → drought conditions → hurts animals → forces nomads _____
3. global warming → _____ days are increasing
4. drought conditions → dry the _____ → stunt the _____ of vegetation → not enough to
   _____ the animals

D Read this passage from the video. Match the underlined words to their definitions below.

There are still an (1) <u>estimated</u> thirty-three million (2) <u>livestock</u> in Mongolia, more than ten times the number
of people. [One nomad named] Basanjav says he wants his children to (3) <u>maintain</u> the tradition of herding. He
says his father was a herder and that it's important that his grandchildren (4) <u>continue in the same footsteps</u>.
But the (5) <u>odds</u> that his grandchildren will grow up to be nomadic herders and continue this proud Mongolian
tradition are becoming increasingly uncertain.

___ a. likelihood   ___ d. to do the same thing someone did
___ b. animals such as cows and sheep   before you
___ c. approximate   ___ e. to preserve

> **Ask**
> **Answer** Think about where your grandparents and parents have lived and the
> jobs they've had. Are you continuing in their footsteps? Why or why not?
> What are the odds that your children will have a better life than you?

Writing
Write a Summary

A Read this summary of the video on page 32. Then answer the questions.

> Global warming has brought an increase in extreme weather events worldwide. In Mongolia, this is especially true, where average temperatures have risen about two degrees over the last sixty years. Mongolians are used to extreme temperatures, but the changes in climate have been more extreme than ever and that has been disastrous for the nomadic people and their way of life. Nowadays winters see heavier snowfalls and the rains in the summer are much less frequent than they used to be. This is a problem because the drought conditions have dried up the soil so much that the vegetation is dying out. The nomads' livestock cannot survive without enough to eat. Without healthy livestock, many nomads have been forced to give up their traditional nomadic lifestyle and move to the city. Because of this trend, global warming may ultimately lead to the destruction of the nomadic way of life.

1. What is the main idea and the conclusion of the paragraph? Underline each sentence.
2. What kind of information did the writer give to move from the main idea to the conclusion?

B Now look back at the article on page 31 and choose an answer to each question. You will use these sentences to start and end your summary.

1. What is the main idea of the article? (paragraph 1) Between 1960 and 2000 . . .
   a. South Korea became more urbanized and the quality of life declined.
   b. South Korea went from being a poor, rural-based economy to a successful urban one.
2. What does the writer conclude? (paragraph 7) A poor country . . .
   a. needs to grow slowly and carefully.
   b. can urbanize successfully and incredibly fast.

C How did the author move from the main idea to the conclusion? What kind of information did the author give? Follow these steps.

1. Use some of these key words to help you find important information and underline it in the article.

wars	education	corporations	infrastructure
housing	transportation	street life	overall health

2. Decide which information you want to include in your summary and then read the Writing Strategy.

> **Writing Strategy**   **Guidelines on Summary Writing** A summary is a shorter account of an original text. It gives a reader a general idea of the text's content. When writing your summary . . .
>
> 1. Don't copy the author's ideas exactly. Rephrase the language with your own words.
> 2. Don't insert your own opinions into it.
> 3. Don't assume your audience already knows about the topic. (You may need to "state the obvious.")

D Use the information in Exercises **B** and **C** and the Writing Strategy to write your summary. Use a separate piece of paper. When you finish, exchange papers with a partner and read their summary. Was your partner's summary clear and concise?

Speaking

A Read this information about life in rural areas fifty years ago and today. What changes have occurred? Discuss with a partner.

> In 2007, it was reported that for the first time in history more than half the global population lived in cities as opposed to rural areas.

FIFTY YEARS AGO

- The average farm was owned and operated by one family. Each farm required a large number of strong men and women to grow enough food to support the family.
- Many young people went directly to work after they graduated from high school.
- Several generations of a family lived and stayed in the village.
- Men and women got married within the same or nearby communities.

TODAY

- Farms are operated by large corporations. Modern farming uses machines and much less human labor.
- Young people need to get a college degree to succeed in the workplace and often leave home to study.
- The younger generations move to bigger cities to look for work.
- It can be harder to find a suitable partner in a small town.

B There are many factors that "push" a person to leave a small town and "pull" a person to migrate to a big city. Read the factors below. Brainstorm with a partner and add others on a separate piece of paper.

PUSH FACTORS (from a smaller town)	PULL FACTORS (to a bigger city)
Not enough jobs	*Better job opportunities*

C You and your partner are urban planners. Come up with a plan for reversing rural flight (the movement from rural areas to a big city).

- Look at your push and pull factors. Choose one to work on.
- On a separate piece of paper, come up with at least three ideas to address the problem.

D Find another pair and take turns presenting your ideas.

> Unlike the cities, the rural district is not crowded with young people seeking work. To attract young workers back to the countryside, we propose. . .

Expanding Your Fluency

A These are photos of a city that has gone through rapid urbanization. Look at the photos and answer the questions with a partner.

1. The name of the city pictured is Astana. Where do you think it is located?
2. What do you think it is known for?
3. What symbol is this city associated with? What does the symbol mean?
4. Do you think this is a livable city? Why or why not?
5. What kinds of things do you think the city's inhabitants do in their free time?
6. What would you be interested in doing there?

B Work with a partner to create a short ad that will be used to attract visitors to Astana. Use some of these words in your ad.

community	district	global	livable	transformation
cosmopolitan	dynamic	infrastructure	metropolitan	urbanization

C Join another pair and take turns reading your ads. What do you like about each one? Why?

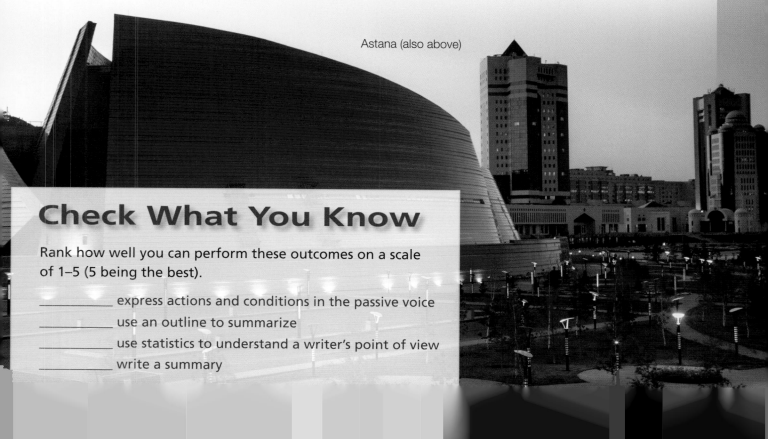

Astana (also above)

Check What You Know

Rank how well you can perform these outcomes on a scale of 1–5 (5 being the best).

_____ express actions and conditions in the passive voice

_____ use an outline to summarize

_____ use statistics to understand a writer's point of view

_____ write a summary

4 Being Yourself

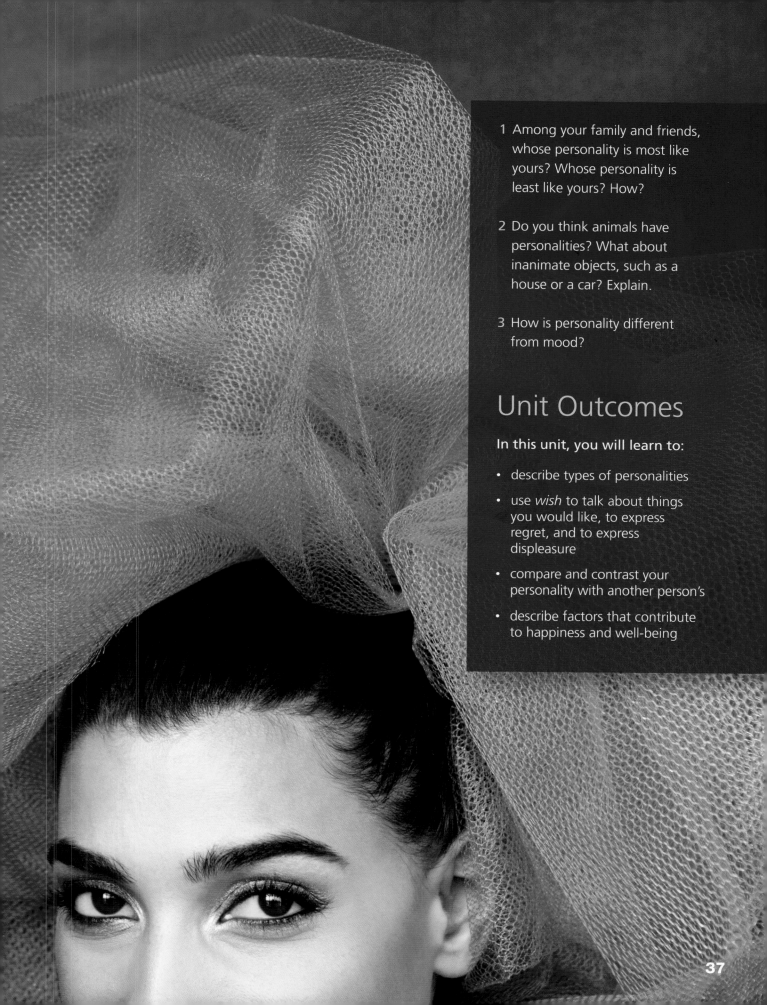

1 Among your family and friends, whose personality is most like yours? Whose personality is least like yours? How?

2 Do you think animals have personalities? What about inanimate objects, such as a house or a car? Explain.

3 How is personality different from mood?

Unit Outcomes

In this unit, you will learn to:

- describe types of personalities

- use *wish* to talk about things you would like, to express regret, and to express displeasure

- compare and contrast your personality with another person's

- describe factors that contribute to happiness and well-being

Vocabulary

affectionate loving and warm

ambitious very motivated to succeed

demanding difficult; insisting that something be done your way

get along (with someone) to have a friendly relationship with someone else

idealistic hopeful; believing in the best

innovative creative; original; inventive; new

picky critical; hard to please; choosy

pushover a person who is easily influenced by others

reserved keeping one's own feelings hidden

sensible logical; realistic

stubborn inflexible; unwilling to change your mind

supportive helpful and kind to those in need

thorough careful; detailed

upbeat positive and cheerful

Usage: It's common to strengthen or soften personality adjectives using modifiers. Words like *really, pretty, so,* and *such* emphasize a word. (*She's pretty upbeat. He's such a pushover.*) It's common to soften negative words that describe people (e.g., *demanding, picky*) with modifiers like *kind of, sort of, a bit, a little,* and *somewhat.*

Innovators: Steve Wozniak (lef and Steve Jobs, inventors of A

A With your class, look at the six personality types below. Match each type (A–F) with a description (1–6). More than one answer is possible.

_____ 1. is motivated to succeed

_____ 2. likes to fix all mistakes

_____ 3. likes caring for others

_____ 4. sees only the best side of things

_____ 5. loves taking risks

_____ 6. is studious and thoughtful

A. The Perfectionist sensible and thorough, but can be picky	**B. The Nurturer** affectionate and supportive, but can be a pushover	**C. The Go-Getter** ambitious and upbeat, but can be demanding
D. The Romantic idealistic and innovative, but can be impractical	**E. The Philosopher** patient and wise, but can seem reserved	**F. The Daredevil** daring and self-confident, but can be stubborn

B Read about the six personality types. Then answer the questions with a partner.

1. Which personality types might get along well with each other? Which might not? Why?

2. Which personality types best describe you? Choose two. Which one least describes you? Explain your choices. How similar are you to your partner?

3. Think of someone you admire; it can be someone you know or someone famous. Which personality type(s) describe that person? How do you compare to that person?

38

Grammar

> **bully** using one's strength or power to hurt or frighten others   **tolerant** accepting and open-minded

Making Wishes

> For *be*, use *were* with both singular and plural subjects. In everyday spoken English, *was* is also used.

	Real Situation	Ideal Situation
❶ **about the present**	I**'m** kind of short.	I wish (that) I **were** taller.
	I **don't speak** French.	I wish (that) I **spoke** French.
	She **has to leave** the party now.	She wishes (that) she **didn't have to leave**.
❷ **about the past**	I **was** careless on the exam.	I wish (that) I **had been** more thorough!
❸ **with** *would*	We can't hear the teacher.	We wish (that) the teacher **would speak** louder so we could hear him.

Use *wish* to . . .
❶ talk about something you would like. In the *that* clause, the verb is in a past form.
❷ express regret about something that happened. In the *that* clause, the verb is in the past perfect.
❸ express displeasure in the moment with something or someone and to say that you want it to change.

Pop singer Lady Gaga (right) started an organization called the Born This Way Foundation. As a teenager, she was bullied by neighborhood kids and classmates. The experience affected her deeply and influenced who she is today. The goals of her foundation are to discourage bullying and encourage people to be supportive and accepting of others.

A Read the information above about Lady Gaga.
Then do the following:

a. Complete sentences 1–5 with the correct form of the verb in parentheses. In some cases, more than one option is possible.

b. Check answers with a partner. Which of the comments do you agree with or relate to? Why?

> **@JustMagical** I was kind of a shy, reserved kid. I wish this foundation (1. be) _____ around when I was in high school!   7:38pm • 3 Apr

> **@tumtumtree72** Lady Gaga is being a little idealistic. I wish people (2. be) _____ kinder to each other, but usually they're not. It's human nature.   7:42pm • 3 Apr

> **@dudberry** I love her idea. I wish more people (3. think) _____ like Lady Gaga! And I wish she (had) (4. create) _____ this foundation sooner! I wish more parents (5. teach) _____ their kids to be respectful and tolerant of others.   7:50pm • 3 Apr

B Discuss the questions.

1. Do you think your personality has been shaped by events in your life? Explain.
2. What about your personality do you like the most? What parts do you wish were different?
3. What's something you wish you had or hadn't done in the past? Why?

Being Yourself   **39**

Listening

be hard on (someone) to treat someone in a severe or unkind way

lab partner in a science class like biology or chemistry, the student you work with in the laboratory to do certain experiments or exercises

work (something) out to find a solution to a problem

A You are going to hear a college student named Alana talk about a chemistry class she is taking. Have you ever taken a chemistry class? Describe it. Did you like it? Why or why not? Discuss with a partner.

B Listen as Alana talks to a friend. Then discuss the questions with a partner.

1. In general, how would you say Alana is doing in school? What kind of student would you say she is? Why?
2. How do you think Alana feels about her chemistry class: upbeat, confused, hopeful, overwhelmed?

TIP Notice how these expressions are used by the speakers: *It's stressing me out.* and *It's driving me crazy.* What feeling(s) do these expressions communicate?

C Read the statements. Then listen again and circle the correct answer.

1. Alana **is / isn't** happy with her most recent chemistry test grade.
   Reason: _____

2. Overall, Alana really **likes / dislikes** her chemistry class.
   Reason: _____

3. Alana wishes she didn't have to work with a **teacher / lab partner**.
   Reason: _____

4. Alana feels that her teacher **has / hasn't** been very supportive and helpful.
   Reason: _____

5. Alana plans to **do more / take a break from** schoolwork tonight.
   Reason: _____

6. The man encourages Alana to **sleep / study more** tonight.
   Reason: _____

D Listen again and give a reason for each statement in Exercise **C**.

E Compare answers in Exercises **C** and **D** with a partner. Then summarize what Alana's problem is. If you were in Alana's situation, what would you do?

40   Unit 4

Connections

A Get into a group of three. Read the information and the three profiles below. Then answer these questions:

1. What problem is the team having? Why aren't they getting along?
2. In general, what sort of personality type(s) would you say each person has?

You work for an international magazine that's published on the first of each month. Your team is responsible for next month's magazine cover and the main article. You are behind schedule because you are all having difficulty working with each other.

project manager You're responsible for getting the project done well and on time. You try to be supportive of your colleagues, but you're feeling a little annoyed with both of them at the moment. For example, you often ask the photographer for one kind of photo, and then he/she gives you something else. You wish he/she listened better. Having to do things over and over is slowing everything down and costing money. The designer has good ideas, though he/she is a bit reserved. You wish he/she would defend his/her ideas more.

photographer You're trying to take innovative, interesting photos for this month's main article and cover, but the project manager keeps telling you to change them. Sure, you don't follow instructions *exactly*. As an artist, you need to be creative in your photography. You wish the project manager were a little more flexible and a little less picky! You've also argued with the designer about which photo should appear on next month's cover. You want one thing, and the designer insists on something else. You wish that he/she weren't so stubborn.

designer You're responsible for the layout of the images on the magazine cover and in the main article. In your opinion, the photographer has taken some interesting photos for next month's cover, but many are impractical. They just won't fit and look good. You really hate arguing and wish the photographer would be reasonable. You've tried talking to the project manager about this, but he/she can be such a pushover and always does whatever the photographer wants. You wish the manager took your side once in a while.

B With your group, decide which role each group member will take. On your own, think about these questions:

1. What do you want from the two other team members?
2. What can you suggest to improve the team's working relationship so that you can complete your project on time?

C Imagine that you and your colleagues are meeting to discuss the problem. Take turns explaining in your own words what issues you're having with the others on your team and what you'd like from them. Together, try to reach a compromise. Make a plan for how you're going to finalize the cover and the main article.

D What compromise did your group reach and how are you all going to move forward? Share your plan with another group. Were your ideas similar?

> Carlos, you've taken some great photos, but I'm worried that they won't look good on the cover. I really wish we didn't have to argue about this. Paloma, you're the project manager, what do you suggest?

Reading

A Make a list of three things that make you happy. Then get into a group of four and compare your answers. Were any of your answers the same? Share your results with the class.

B Read only the title and the first paragraph of the article. Then guess where the happiest place in Asia, Europe, and the Americas is. Why do you think people there are happy? Compare your ideas with a partner's. Then read the rest of the article to check your ideas.

C Locate the word or phrase in the paragraph noted in the chart. In the same paragraph, find the synonym or antonym of the word or phrase and write it in the chart.

Paragraph	Word or phrase	Synonym	Antonym
1	satisfaction (*noun*)	_____	unhappiness
2	peace of mind (*noun*)	_____	danger
3	honesty (*noun*)	truthfulness	_____
3	tolerance (*noun*)	acceptance	_____

D Complete the graphic organizer with information from the article. List the country or region and the reasons why these are the happiest places on Earth. Then summarize the findings with a partner.

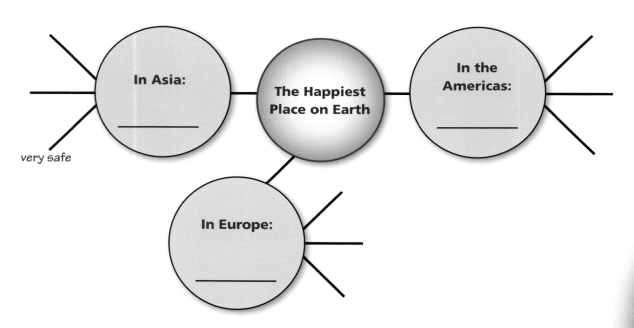

In Asia:
_____
very safe

The Happiest Place on Earth

In the Americas:
_____

In Europe:
_____

E Discuss the questions with a partner.

1. Did any of the findings in the article surprise you?
2. How does your country or region compare to those listed in the article? In general, would you say that people where you live are happy? Why or why not? Which of the "happiness factors" in Exercise **D** do you wish were more common in your country?

SECRETS of the Happiest Places on Earth

1   For much of the last decade, author and explorer Dan Buettner has traveled to places where people live longest and where they claim to get the greatest satisfaction from their lives. Recently, Buettner visited different continents and worked with leading researchers to identify the happiest place on each. Where are these places, why are people there happier than others, and what can we learn from these people about finding contentment in our own lives? Dan Buettner's findings may surprise you.

Asia

Most people believe the happiest place in Asia is Bhutan. It's not. According to research, it's Singapore, for a variety of reasons. First, Singapore is very safe. A woman can walk alone at night without the fear of being harmed. Children can spend time at the playground and parents don't have to worry about them being taken. This peace of mind is very important when it comes to happiness. Also, 90% of Singaporeans own their own home—another source of security. There are also tax incentives[1] to live close to your aging parents, so seniors are taken care of at a higher level. Research shows that we're happier when we socialize, and we get the most satisfaction from socializing with our families.

Europe

Worldwide, happiness correlates[2] very strongly with equality. Countries that have a very narrow gap between the richest and the poorest people are a lot happier than those where only a few people make a lot of money and the others don't make much. In Denmark, a CEO only makes about three times as much as an average worker, whereas in other countries, CEOs make many thousands of times as much as a typical employee. Research also shows that honesty and trust strongly correlate with happiness. Places where people are honest and where there is low governmental corruption tend to be happier. Tolerance also contributes to contentment. Knowing that you won't face discrimination because of your gender, age, religious beliefs, or ethnicity makes people happier. All three of these things promote a sense of well-being and are present in Denmark, making it the happiest place in Europe.

The Americas

Buettner also looked at Nuevo León, the happiest region of Mexico, which was the happiest country in the American hemisphere when he did his research. Something interesting is going on in this part of Mexico. Research shows that worldwide, religious people are happier than nonreligious people, and for more than 80% of those in Nuevo León, religious faith tops their list of values. Family is also extremely important in Nuevo León; this includes not only moms, dads, and children; but also aunts, uncles, cousins, and grandparents. Having a large extended family does some helpful things, such as providing a financial safety net,[3] which is a defense against stress. Of course, people in Mexico do suffer from all kinds of difficult things in their lives, but a large family can be supportive and help a person get through the challenging times. Also, there are many weddings, birthday parties, and other family events that people attend; this means that residents of Nuevo León are getting lots of social interaction, which contributes a lot to personal happiness.

[1] **tax incentive** a decrease in the amount of tax one must pay
[2] **correlate** to have a close connection to something else
[3] **safety net** money you can rely on if you get into a difficult financial situation

Singapore, one of the happiest places in the world

Video

longevity long life
obesity the state of being very overweight
sedentary inactive; sitting a lot
unplug to relax and do nothing
wear the pants to be in control
zeal a strong enthusiasm for something

A Discuss the questions with a partner.

1. Who is the oldest person you know? How has he or she managed to live so long?

2. Researcher David McLain visited three "cultures of longevity." What do you know about the three places in Exercise **B**? Why do you think people there are living so long?

B Read the information below and then watch the video. Complete each aging fact. Then match the reasons (a–e) with a place. A reason can be used more than once.

Place	Aging fact	Reason(s) people live so long
Sardinia, Italy	Men there live _____ women.	
Okinawa, Japan	Okinawa is home to the _____ on Earth.	
Loma Linda, USA	Seventh-day Adventists outlive other Americans by _____ years.	

Reasons people live so long:

a. They have active lifestyles.
b. They regularly take a day off.
c. They have lower stress levels (especially the men).
d. They socialize with family or friends often.
e. They have a healthy diet.

? **Did you know?**

On average, women tend to live five years longer than men.

C Compare answers in Exercise **B** with a partner. Explain what information from the video helped you choose your answers for each place.

D In each place, is the culture of longevity changing? Watch the video again. Mark *yes* or *no* and list the reason(s).

Sardinia   yes / no   reason: _____

Okinawa   yes / no   reason: _____

Loma Linda   yes / no   reason: _____

E Discuss these questions with a partner.

1. Why are the people in each place living so long? Were any of the reasons for longevity the same?

2. Which factors mentioned in the video were also mentioned in the reading on page 43? What does this tell us about the connection between happiness and long life?

Speaking

A Complete the survey by marking how you feel on the scale. Are you closer to one side or the other, or are you in the middle? Be prepared to explain your responses.

Life Satisfaction Survey

I'm feeling stressed out by life at the moment.	1 2 3 4 5	I'm pretty upbeat about most things in my life.
I wish I lived somewhere else.	1 2 3 4 5	I like where I live.
My family drives me crazy.	1 2 3 4 5	I get along well with my family members.
I wish I were a more social person.	1 2 3 4 5	I have a decent social life.
I wish school wasn't so hard./ I wish I had a different job.	1 2 3 4 5	I like the school I go to or the job I do.
I'd like to change some things about my appearance.	1 2 3 4 5	I'm satisfied with my appearance.

B Get together with a partner and do the following:

1. On a separate piece of paper, draw a diagram like the one shown. Make it large enough to fit your responses and your partner's responses.

2. With your partner, compare your responses to the survey in Exercise **A**. Record your answers and your partner's answers in the diagram. Remember to explain your answers. Take notes on what your partner tells you.

3. Discuss the questions. Use the language in the Speaking Strategy.

   • In general, how similar are you to each other?

   • Are there things your partner wishes he or she could change?

   • What advice can you suggest?

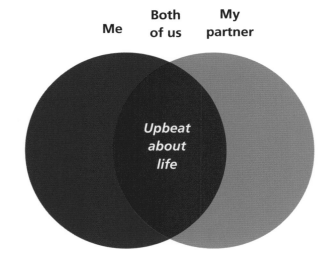

Me	Both of us	My partner
	Upbeat about life	

Speaking Strategy	**Making General Comparisons**	**Making Specific Comparisons**
	We're fundamentally/completely different.	I'm pretty upbeat about most things in my life.
	We're kind of/sort of/somewhat similar.	Yeah, me too./So am I.
	We're very similar./We're pretty much alike.	I'm kind of in the middle.
	We're virtually/practically/almost identical.	Not me. I'm feeling really stressed out by school these days.

Writing
Compare and Contrast Yourself with Another Person

A Read the paragraphs. Then answer the questions below with the same partner you worked with on page 45.

> For the most part, my partner Mayumi and I are very similar. For example, we're **both** pretty upbeat people. She's almost always in a good mood and **so am I. Like me,** she rarely gets stressed out or lets little things get her down. Mayumi gets along well with her family members and **the same is true for** me. Mayumi is close to her younger sister, and I'm especially close to my mom and brother.
>
> Both Mayumi and I are also very social people and enjoy hanging out with our friends; **however,** we don't really like doing the same things. She loves going out to clubs on the weekends. I, **on the other hand,** prefer to relax or play video games with my friends. Mayumi also goes out a lot and has a pretty decent social life, **whereas** I wish I had more free time. Going to school and working a part-time job make that difficult, though. Despite these minor differences, Mayumi and I are very similar.

Start the composition with a clear topic sentence that states generally how you and your partner compare.

Illustrate each point of similarity or difference with extra facts or information.

End with a sentence that summarizes how you and your partner compare.

1. How are the writer and Mayumi similar? How are they different?
2. Which boldfaced words or phrases compare? Which contrast? Answer on a separate piece of paper.

B You are going to write a short composition comparing yourself to your partner. Follow these steps.

1. Outline your ideas.
   a. Start with a topic sentence that states generally how you and your partner compare.
   b. Using the diagram and the notes you took on page 45, identify three points of similarity or difference that support your topic sentence.
   c. Illustrate each point of similarity or difference with extra facts or information.
   d. Conclude with a sentence that summarizes how you and your partner compare.

2. Use your outline to write your composition. Remember to use the boldfaced words and phrases from Exercise **A**.

C Exchange papers with a different partner and read the other student's composition. Does it achieve the four things listed in Exercise **B1** (a–d) and use the boldfaced words and phrases?

Expanding Your Fluency

A Take two slips of paper. On each, write a wish about your personality. Then give them to your teacher.

> I wish that I were more ambitious.

> I wish I was a little less demanding.

> I wish I weren't such a perfectionist sometimes.

> I wish I were more supportive with friends.

B   Your teacher will now give you two slips of paper. Find who wrote each wish. When you find the person, ask him or her to explain why he/she made that wish. Take notes on what the person tells you.

> Do you wish you were more ambitious?

> Yeah, I wrote that.

> Why did you make that wish?

> Sometimes I lack confidence . . .

Rub the lamp and you will be granted three wishes.

C Get together with a partner and describe the two wishes you learned about. Of the four wishes you two have in total, which <u>one</u> would you grant if you could? Why? Share your answer with the class.

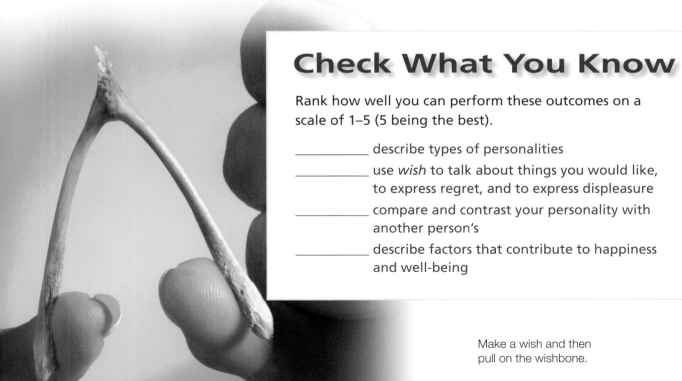

Check What You Know

Rank how well you can perform these outcomes on a scale of 1–5 (5 being the best).

_____ describe types of personalities

_____ use *wish* to talk about things you would like, to express regret, and to express displeasure

_____ compare and contrast your personality with another person's

_____ describe factors that contribute to happiness and well-being

Make a wish and then pull on the wishbone.

5 Mystery Solved!

1 Where do you think this statue is located? How do you think it got there? Do you think it's mysterious? Why or why not?

2 What is the strangest animal you have ever seen or read about?

3 Name three places on Earth that are considered mysterious. Which one would you most like to visit? Why?

Unit Outcomes

In this unit, you will learn to:

- use modals of possibility in the past, present, and future

- speculate about mysteries

- refute ideas

- use *wh-* questions to help you plan a story

Vocabulary

absorb to reduce the force of something; soak up or take in

aggressive acting in an angry or violent manner

case a situation or incident

clue something that helps you find the answer to a problem

mystery something that is difficult to understand or explain

observation the act of carefully watching someone or something

solve to find an answer to a problem or crime

surroundings the immediate area around you

theory a formal idea that is intended to explain something

twist to turn •——

uncover to discover something previously unknown or hidden

unharmed not hurt or damaged in any way

> **Usage:** *Twist* is a verb, but it can also be used as a noun as it is below in **bold**. What is the meaning of that usage of *twi*

A Use words from the list to complete the two stories below.
🙎 Work with a partner.

Animal Mysteries

Sam the Parrot

Parrots are popular pets because they're friendly and intelligent.

Sandy, who recently married Ken, has a parrot named Sam. Sam was a loving pet . . . until about six months ago. He became (1) _____ and started biting Ken. Sandy can't understand why Sam has changed from a loving pet to an attack bird. There are few (2) _____ to explain Sam's behavior.

Can you help Sandy by solving this (3) _____?

PARROT FACTS:
- Parrots can "talk" (say short words) like people do. They do this to fit into new (4) _____.
- Parrots form close pair bonds. In the wild, a parrot couple can stay together for decades.
- We know that parrots feel that "three's a crowd."

Acrobatic Cats

We all know from personal (5) _____ that when cats fall, they almost always land on their feet. There are stories of cats surviving long falls out of building windows virtually (6) _____.

There's a **twist** to this story, though. In a recent study, veterinarian Michael Garvey (7) _____ a mystery about cats. He discovered that cats that fall a longer distance have fewer injuries than cats that fall shorter distances.

CAT FACTS:
- When cats fall, the first thing they do is twist their heads around quickly to straighten their bodies.
- Then, they completely relax their bodies.
- Finally, they land on all four feet in order to (8) _____ the impact.

B Work with a partner and answer the two questions below. Come
🙎 up with a theory for each mystery.

1. Why did Sam's behavior suddenly change?
2. Why do cats that fall shorter distances have more injuries?

Grammar

You're going to the zoo. You've agreed to meet Joe and Ann there at 9:45 a.m. Read the sentences in the chart below to see what happens.

Modals of Possibility in the Past, Present, and Future

	Present/Future	Past
strong certainty	(9:45 a.m.) Joe's not here yet. He **must** be on his way, though.	(9:45 a.m.) Ann's not here yet. She **must have** left her house late.
weaker certainty	(9:50 a.m.) He's still not here. He **could/may/might** be stuck in traffic.	(9:50 a.m.) She's still not here. I **could have/may have/might have** told her the wrong time.
impossibility	(9:58 a.m.) He just got here. I **can't/couldn't** be more relieved.	(the next day) Ann said she didn't see me at the zoo. She **couldn't have** looked very hard—I was there the whole time!

A Read about this animal mystery and then mark your answers below.

Possible causes of population decline: pollution, climate change, loss of habitat, rise in human population, disease

Animal Mystery: Frogs Disappearing

Scientists have observed something shocking among frog populations worldwide. Out of 6,000 frog species, one-third are facing massive decline. No one is certain why this is happening, but we do know that frogs are very sensitive to their surroundings—especially to changes in the air and water.

Here's what different people had to say about the situation:

1. "I was shocked to hear that most of the frogs in this area have died out. That just **can't / must** be true!"

2. "With all the research tools we have, I'm certain we can figure this out. There **might / must** be a simple answer to this mystery."

3. "I can't find any frogs today. At first, I thought they **might / might not** be hiding. But now I know that isn't true."

4. "It's pretty obvious that humans are at fault. We **couldn't have / must have** done something to damage the environment . . . and that's killing off the frogs."

5. "Some people say that dogs and cats killed all the frogs in this area, but that **could have / couldn't have** been the only cause."

B   Why do you think that frogs are disappearing worldwide? Read the possible causes in Exercise **A**. Discuss each cause with a partner.

> I think pollution could be one of the causes. It says that frogs are sensitive to . . .

Ask

Answer Are there any mysteries where you live that people can't explain? If so, what are they? Are there any clues or do you have any theories about them?

Listening

tow to pull something or someone by a rope tied to a vehicle

Talking about groups of animals
a herd of cattle
a pod of dolphins
a school of fish

A Look at the information in the box and the photo. You are going to hear a story about Erik. What do you think happened to Erik? Discuss with a partner.

B Listen to the news story about what happened to Erik. Complete the sentences below. You will not hear all of the answers.

1. where he surfs   *He surfs at _____.*
2. what the doctors expect   *They expect him to make a complete _____.*
3. why he was so far away   *He was _____ out to sea by a jet ski.*
4. what happened to him   *He was _____ by a _____.*
5. what happened to his surfboard   *The _____ bit it.*
6. who helped him   *A _____ of _____ helped him.*
7. how they helped him   *They _____ around him and _____ him.*

C Now listen to two friends talking about Erik. Complete the rest of the sentences in Exercise **B**.

D Listen and complete the expressions that express shock and disbelief/surprise.

Expressing shock	Expressing disbelief/surprise
This _____ as a complete shock.	I just _____ how scared he must have been.
I was _____ to hear the news . . .	_____ that he was able to escape.

E Work with a partner. Close your books and practice retelling Erik's story. Use one of the expressions in Exercise **D** and some of the words below.

aggressive   mystery   observation   twist   unharmed

Ask

Answer Do you believe Erik's story? Why or why not?
Why do you think the dolphins helped Erik? Do you know any other stories where animals helped humans?

A surfer on his surfboard

Connections

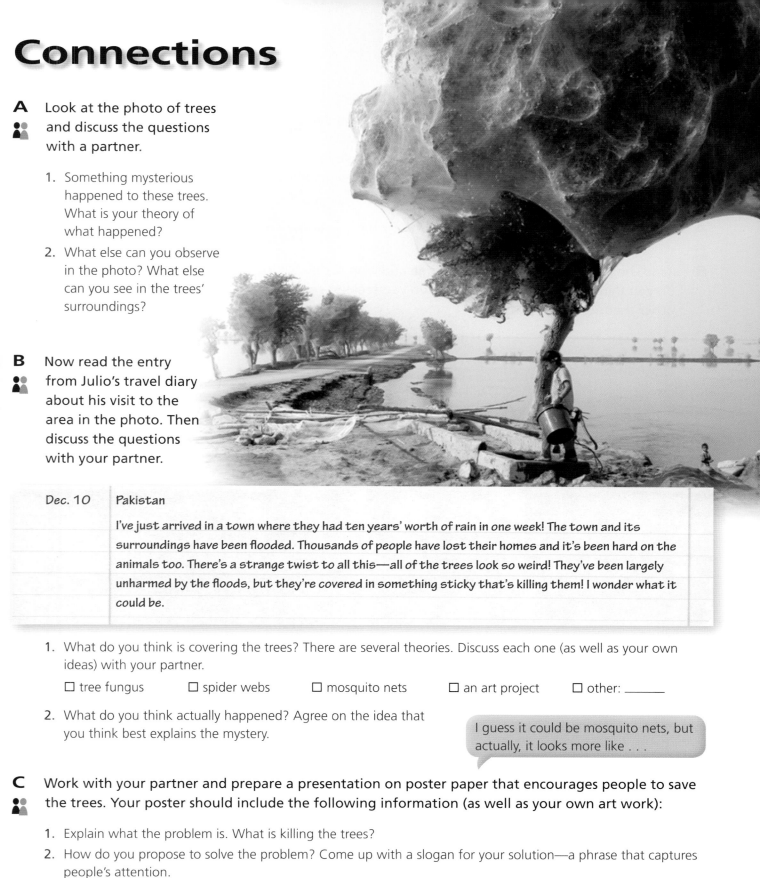

A Look at the photo of trees and discuss the questions with a partner.

1. Something mysterious happened to these trees. What is your theory of what happened?

2. What else can you observe in the photo? What else can you see in the trees' surroundings?

B Now read the entry from Julio's travel diary about his visit to the area in the photo. Then discuss the questions with your partner.

Dec. 10	Pakistan
	I've just arrived in a town where they had ten years' worth of rain in one week! The town and its surroundings have been flooded. Thousands of people have lost their homes and it's been hard on the animals too. There's a strange twist to all this—all of the trees look so weird! They've been largely unharmed by the floods, but they're covered in something sticky that's killing them! I wonder what it could be.

1. What do you think is covering the trees? There are several theories. Discuss each one (as well as your own ideas) with your partner.

   ☐ tree fungus   ☐ spider webs   ☐ mosquito nets   ☐ an art project   ☐ other: _____

2. What do you think actually happened? Agree on the idea that you think best explains the mystery.

> I guess it could be mosquito nets, but actually, it looks more like . . .

C Work with your partner and prepare a presentation on poster paper that encourages people to save the trees. Your poster should include the following information (as well as your own art work):

1. Explain what the problem is. What is killing the trees?

2. How do you propose to solve the problem? Come up with a slogan for your solution—a phrase that captures people's attention.

D Present your ideas to the class. The class votes on the best presentation.

Speaking

> **bury** to place something in a hole in the ground and cover it with dirt
>
> **cemetery** a place where the bodies or ashes of the dead are buried
>
> **monument** a large structure, usually made of stone, built to remind people of something
>
> **skeleton** the frame of bones supporting a human or animal body

A Look at the photos below. Tell your partner what you know about them.

B Read the information about Stonehenge and crop circles. Which theory do you think is correct for each? Why do you feel less confident in the other theories?

Circular Mysteries of the World

STONEHENGE

Stonehenge is an ancient site made up of large stones arranged in a circle.

Constructed:
3100 BCE–1600 BCE

Builders: unknown

What is it? Theories:
1. Ancient people might have placed the stones carefully to use as a kind of calendar.
2. Scientists have discovered skeletons buried on the site. They think it may have been a cemetery.
3. Some of the skeletons have strange wounds. People may have come to Stonehenge to get medical treatment.
4. The nearby residents may have arranged the stones to create a monument of peace and unity.

CROP CIRCLES

Crop circles are large areas of flattened crops in the shape of various patterns.

First noticed: 1970s

Builders: unknown

How are they made? Theories:
1. Scientists wonder if strange weather patterns might have caused the circles to form.
2. Some say the patterns can easily be made using a rope and board to crush the crops.
3. Some claim that aliens created the circles as directions for an invasion of Earth.
4. Some scientists have suggested that you can create the patterns by "burning" the fields with lasers.

C Follow these steps with your partner.

1. Student A: State which Stonehenge theory you believe.
2. Student A: Take no more than one minute to refute the other theories. Use the Speaking Strategy to help you explain why the theories are wrong.
3. Student B: After Student A finishes, complete steps 1 and 2.
4. Students A and B: Discuss which arguments were most convincing.
5. Students A and B: Follow steps 1–4 with the crop circle theories.

> **Speaking Strategy**
>
> **Refuting a Theory**
>
> *Moderate*
>
> *It's possible that _____.*
> *However, it's more likely that _____ because . . .*
> *I suppose that _____ could be true, but that's probably not the case because . . .*
>
> ***Stronger***
>
> *It seems unlikely that . . .*
> *I doubt (very much) that . . .*
> *It's impossible that . . .*
> *There's no chance that . . .*

Video

archaeologist a person who studies people and societies of the past by examining their culture, architecture, tools, and other objects

complex a group of buildings designed for a particular purpose

loot to steal from shops and houses

settlement a place where people gather to build homes and live

withstand to survive or not give in to a force or action

A Match the words in the box with their antonym. Use your dictionary to help you.

| isolated | novel | permanent | solitary |

1. temporary _____
2. easy to reach _____
3. unoriginal _____
4. together (with other things) _____

B What do you think Stonehenge may have been used for? Think back to the answer you gave on page 54. Watch the video and complete the sentences.

According to an archaeologist, Stonehenge was not a / an (1) _____ monument. People lived in (2) _____ homes nearby and (3) _____ their (4) _____ at Stonehenge.

PRONUNCIATION

Is Michael Parker Pearson's accent American or British? How can you tell? For more on the differences between American English and British English, see p. 145.

C Watch the video about Stonehenge and a nearby settlement called Durrington Walls. Match each description with one of the locations.

	Stonehenge	Durrington Walls
1. has been looted.	☐	☐
2. was a large community.	☐	☐
3. is an obsession for Mr. Pearson, an archaeologist.	☐	☐
4. is located upstream.	☐	☐
5. is not a solitary, isolated place.	☐	☐
6. was where people lived.	☐	☐
7. was where people were buried.	☐	☐
8. is timeless.	☐	☐

D Each sentence has one error. Watch the video and correct the sentences.

1. Archaeologist Michael Parker Pearson has been digging around Stonehenge since 1999.
2. In 2006, he made a great discovery of many skeletons.
3. Durrington Walls may have contained dozens of houses.
4. It is estimated that 240 stones were placed at Stonehenge.

Ask

Answer What do you think of Michael Parker Pearson's theory? Do you think Stonehenge is a mysterious place? Why or why not?

Reading

A Read the title and subtitle of the article and look at the map.

Who do you think would visit Stonehenge 3,500 years ago? Tell a partner what you think.

Great Britain

Stonehenge

B Find the word or phrase that matches the definition.

1. _____ (paragraph 3) unusual and interesting, often because it comes from a distant country
2. _____ (paragraph 4) to reduce the number of choices or ideas
3. _____ (paragraph 5) data that represents a person's traits
4. _____ (paragraph 7) made guesses about something
5. _____ (paragraph 8) a disease caused by germs or bacteria

Amber beads

C Why does the writer mention these place names in the article? Read the article and make notes about each place on a separate piece of paper.

1. Mediterranean coast
2. Amesbury
3. English Channel

D What do scientists know about the boy with the amber necklace? What do those facts tell us about him? Read the article again and complete the chart.

Clue	What we know	What it tells us
Teeth		
Necklace		
Age		
Injuries		

Ask

Answer Do you know of any places that contain mysteries like Stonehenge? Have the mysteries been solved? What clues were left?

The Boy with the Amber Necklace

3,500 years ago, Stonehenge was attracting visitors from all over the world. The question is: Who were they?

1 Stonehenge has long been a source of mystery and questions. Who built it? Why did they build it? How was it built? But today, advances in science are beginning to reveal information that could change the way we think about the ancient site. For instance, new evidence shows that Bronze Age[1] people traveled all the way from the Mediterranean coast—more than 500 miles (805 kilometers) away—to see the standing stones on Britain's Salisbury Plain.

10 One notable example of these Bronze Age visitors to Stonehenge is a 14- or 15-year-old boy buried outside the town of Amesbury, about 3 miles (5 kilometers) from Stonehenge. Chemical analysis of his teeth reveal that he came from somewhere in the Mediterranean region.

Discovered in 2005, the teen was buried about 3,550 years ago wearing a necklace of about 90 amber[2] beads. "Such exotic materials demonstrate that he was from one of the highest levels of society," said project archaeologist Andrew Fitzpatrick of Wessex Archaeology,
20 a consulting firm based in Salisbury, England.

To determine that the teen wasn't a local, scientists from the British Geological[3] Survey (BGS) measured oxygen[4] and other substances in his teeth. The amounts of these substances change depending on an area's unique climate and geology. This information gets recorded in a person's teeth and can be used to narrow down their native region.

In the case of the boy with the amber necklace, it became clear that he wasn't originally from Stonehenge.
30 Instead, his chemical profile matched that of a person from an area like the coastal Mediterranean. In short, scientists think he traveled to Stonehenge from a much warmer place.

The researchers were able to learn even more about the boy. Because he was so young, archaeologists suspect the boy traveled with an extended family group. "We think that the wealthiest people may have made these long-distance journeys in order to find rare and exotic materials, like amber. By doing these journeys,
40 they probably also acquired great kudos,"[5] Wessex's Fitzpatrick noted.

Crossing the English Channel from mainland Europe—most likely by paddleboat—was probably one of the more challenging parts of this journey, he speculated.

The boy's skeleton bears no obvious injuries, suggesting he died of infection. He was buried near Stonehenge likely because of its significance at the time, experts say. The boy is just one of a number of burials
50 near Stonehenge that show that the monument drew visitors from far and wide.

[1] **Bronze Age** the period of ancient human culture between 4000 and 1200 BCE
[2] **amber** a hard yellowish-brown substance used to make jewelry
[3] **geological** related to the study of the Earth's rocks, minerals, and surface
[4] **oxygen** a gas in the air that all humans, animals, and plants need to live
[5] **kudos** public admiration or recognition received when doing something

Writing

Recount a Story

A Read the letter from the Bronze Age. Then answer the questions.

Hi and greetings from Britain!   May 17, 2000 BCE

After a weeklong journey from France, my family and I finally arrived in Britain three days ago. The trip could
have been easier, but on the second day, a terrible storm slowed our channel crossing. . . . I've never seen
such big waves! Fortunately, our boat was able to withstand the high winds and rough seas and we arrived
exhausted, but unharmed. I've never been so happy to get somewhere in my life!

   Our journey is just beginning, though. Tomorrow we head out for Stonehenge. It sounds like a mysterious
place, but I really can't be sure. There are all these stones clustered together in different formations. We'll be
staying nearby in Woodhenge. My mother says she must do some shopping while she's here—she wants to
buy some amber stones for her . . .

---

1. Who do you think wrote it?
   a. a servant being taken with a family to Stonehenge
   b. a teenager traveling with his / her family to Stonehenge
   c. a merchant going to Stonehenge to buy exotic jewels to sell in his / her country
2. What do you think the purpose of this letter is?
   a. to describe the journey
   b. to give some practical advice
   c. to complain about something

B Imagine that you are living in ancient times, and you're making a trip to Stonehenge or another
mysterious site. You are going to write a letter back home to a friend. Do the following:

1. Decide which mysterious site you are visiting, who you are, and why you're writing. (What is your purpose?)
   Use the ideas in Exercise **A** or ideas of your own.
2. Read the Writing Strategy. Then complete the organizer with details about your story.
3. Using your notes, write a letter of at least three paragraphs.

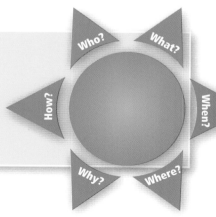

**Writing
Strategy** **Using a Graphic Organizer to Help You Tell a Story**
The graphic organizer to the right can help you to organize your
thoughts before you write. By answering the *wh-* questions in the
organizer, you force yourself to think about all the main details of your story.
1. Write the topic of your letter (trip to a mysterious site) in the middle of the circle.
2. Write *wh-* questions that relate to your topic. You will answer these questions in
   your letter.

C Exchange letters with a partner.

1. Without looking at your partner's organizer, what are some of the questions that his or her letter answers?
   Do you have any unanswered questions?
2. What is the most interesting thing you learned from your partner's letter? The most surprising thing?

Expanding Your Fluency

A   Choose one of the objects in the photos and complete the role-play below.

Archaeologist: You have made a fascinating discovery and are meeting a reporter to tell the world about your exciting discovery. Think about how you would answer the questions from the list.

Reporter: Ask the archaeologist about the object using the questions from the list. You can add some of your own questions to the list.

- Where did you find it?
- Who used it?
- Why is it important?
_____
_____
_____
_____
_____

B   Switch roles and do the role-play again with the other object.

Check What You Know

Rank how well you can perform these outcomes on a scale of 1–5 (5 being the best).

_____ use modals of possibility in the past, present, and future

_____ speculate about mysteries

_____ refute ideas

_____ use *wh-* questions to help you plan a story

6 New Horizons

1 What do you see? What do you think is happening in this photo?

2 What kinds of new discoveries do you think will be made in the future?

3 Flip through the unit quickly. What new possibilities will you be learning about in this unit? Which one looks most interesting to you?

Unit Outcomes

In this unit, you will learn to:

- make predictions using different future forms

- identify key words used to explain reasons

- describe skills needed to achieve future goals

- develop and write a counterargument

74° 45.76' 18
74° 45.72' 18
74° 45.49' 18
73° 35.12' 18
73° 38.29' 18
73° 38.32' 18

Vocabulary

cutting-edge the most advanced or most exciting in a particular field

efficient able to do tasks successfully, without wasting time or energy

feasible possible

interact (with) to communicate as you work or spend time together with others

obsolete no longer necessary because something better has been invented

primitive simple; not well developed

take (something) for granted accept that something is true or normal without thinking about it

versatile able to be used for many different purposes

A What technologies did not exist a hundred years ago that we now take for granted? How have these things transformed people's lives? What would life be like without them? Discuss your answers with a partner.

B Look at the photos and describe what you see. Then use the vocabulary from the list to complete the profile below. Work with a partner.

ROBOT REVOLUTION

Types of robots
android a robot that looks human
drone a robotic flying device

Robots are being created that can think, (1) _____ with people, and even relate to people. Though humanlike robots are still fairly primitive, it's (2) _____ that "in five or ten years androids will routinely be functioning in human environments," says Reid Simmons, a professor of robotics at Carnegie Mellon University. These versatile and (3) _____ machines will cook for us, wash and fold the laundry, and even care for and teach our children while we watch from a computer miles away. Though such technology now seems innovative, by 2100, say scientists, we'll (4) _____ it _____, just like we do driving a car or making a phone call. Other ways that robots might transform our lives:

This robot mimics human gestures, such as shaking hands.

- Robotic autocars will drive for us, which will make the roads safer.

- Microscopic medical "nanobots" will repair old cells and cure diseases, increasing our lives by hundreds of years.

- Flying drones will deliver packages and pizzas right to our doors, making delivery people (5) _____.

C Do you think that using robots will make our lives better? Why or why not? What might be some of the positive and negative consequences? Discuss your answers with a partner.

This drone has a camera and can be used by police.

Grammar

A Study the chart and answer the questions below with a partner.

Predictions with Future Forms

future continuous: Use to show that an event will be ongoing in the future.	*will/be going to* + *be* + present participle ❶ In five or ten years, robots **will be functioning** in human environments.
future perfect: Use to show that a future event will be finished by some future point in time.	*will* + *have* + past participle ❷ By 2020, scientists believe that we **will have found** a cure for certain types of cancer.
future in the past: Use to talk in present time about a prediction that was made in the past.	*would* or *was/were going to* + base form of the verb Carlos thought getting a job after graduation **would be** hard, but he was hired by a company right away.

❶ It would also be correct to use the simple future or *be going to* here. Notice though that the simple future states that an action will or won't happen. The future continuous emphasizes the duration or ongoing status of the action.

❷ This sentence means that at some point before 2020, scientists will discover a cure for cancer. It would also be possible to say here, *We will find a cure for cancer by 2020.*

Which form do we use to talk about . . .

- an ongoing event in the future?
- a prediction that was made previously?
- an event that will be finished at some point in the future?

B Complete the sentences using the correct future form of the verb in parentheses. Sometimes more than one answer is possible. Check your answers with a partner.

1. Over the next decade, more women (enter) _____ the workplace, and many more companies (hire) _____ female managers and CEOs.

2. By the end of the twenty-first century, experts believe we (exhaust) _____ all major oil reserves.

3. In 1900, an American magazine predicted that Russian (be) _____ the second most widely-spoken language in the world after English.

4. Experts believe almost 70% of the world's people (live) _____ in cities by 2050.

5. *Futurist Magazine* predicts that by 2021, commercial space travel (become) _____ very popular and that more than thirteen thousand people (travel) _____ into space.

6. In the late 1960s, artist Andy Warhol said that one day, everyone (have) _____ a chance to be famous for fifteen minutes. Thanks to the Internet, his prediction has come true.

C Make your own prediction about society, fashion, travel, education, work, or another topic, and write it on the board. Then read your classmates' ideas. Which predictions seem feasible? Which don't? Why? Tell a partner.

Ask

Answer Look at the past predictions in Exercise **B**. Can you think of any other predictions that people made in the past that did or didn't come true?

Listening

A At a recent press conference, an aviation expert
answered questions about the future of air travel. Read
the questions below. Do you think the expert will answer
yes or *no*? Why? Tell a partner.

_____ Will we someday commute to work in flying cars?

_____ In the future, will commerical airliners fly faster than
they do now?

_____ Is it possible that we'll ever use jet packs to get around?

Man in
flight using
a jet pack

B Which question is the expert answering? Listen and write
the correct number (1, 2, or 3) next to each question in
Exercise **A**.

C How did the expert actually respond to each question?
Read the Listening Strategy. Then listen again and circle
yes or *no*. Fill in the notes on the reasons he gives for
each response.

Listening Strategy   **Signal Phrases** As you listen, pay attention to how the speaker
uses these signal phrases to explain his reasons: *For a couple
of reasons . . .; One of the main reasons is . . .; There are good
reasons why . . .; Keep in mind, too, that . . .; Another important reason is that . . .*
When you hear these used, be prepared to take notes on what the speaker
says. As you're taking notes, try to list only key words (nouns, verbs, adjectives,
numbers), not every word.

Question	Response	Reasons
1	yes / no	a. The cost of _____ : the more you use, the more _____ a flight is. b. Traveling at _____ speeds isn't _____; the plane can _____ in the air.
2	yes / no	a. An accident would almost always be _____. b. Most models that we have now aren't _____. You can't switch from _____ to _____.
3	yes / no	a. _____ b. _____

D Look back at the reasons you wrote in Exercise **C** and answer the following questions about the
expert's comments with a partner.

1. Which forms of air transportation did people in the past predict we'd have by now?

2. Which one does the expert believe we'll be using in the future? What are some of the current challenges of
using this form of transportation?

3. Were you surprised by any of the expert's answers? Why or why not?

Connections

A Read the predictions below about the workplace. Then answer Questions 1–3 with a partner. When you're done, list your ideas to Questions 2 and 3 on the board.

1. Which items are already common where you live?
2. Can you think of other skills that people will need in the future?
3. What are some things you can do to get the skills needed to succeed in the workplace?

Scientists prepare an experiment using fiber optic cables.

Today's Workplace . . . and Tomorrow's

- People will be changing jobs more often. Fewer people will be staying with one company in the same position for life. Many more people will be freelancing or starting their own businesses.
- People will need to be versatile and efficient—not just good at one thing, but skilled in many different areas.
- Innovative critical thinkers with problem-solving skills will be in demand.
- The ability to interact effectively with others will continue to be in demand, as many more people will be expected to work in teams to get jobs done.
- Those who are fluent in English and at least one other language will be favored over monolingual speakers.
- Your prediction: _____

B On your own, write your answers to the questions below on a separate piece of paper.

1. What is your current occupation? If you are a student, what are you studying?
2. What are some of your short- and long-term career goals? For example, what do you expect you'll be doing a year from now? How about five years from now?
3. How do you plan to accomplish those goals?
4. Do you feel that you have the skills necessary to be successful in tomorrow's workplace? Why or why not? If not, what are you planning to do to improve your skill set?

C Get together with a partner and take turns asking and answering the questions in Exercise **B**. What do you think of your partner's plans? What other suggestions can you give?

> What are some of your short- and long-term career goals?

> A year from now, I'll be applying to graduate school. Five years from now, I will have taken my company public.

D Repeat Exercise **C** with two other partners. Then share the most helpful piece of advice you got with the rest of the class.

Reading

? **Did you know?**

Earth's atmosphere . . .
- provides us with the oxygen we need to breathe.
- protects us from the sun's harmful rays.
- keeps our planet warm enough for plants to grow and for oceans, rivers, and seas to form.

atmosphere layer of air or gas around a planet
habitable good enough for people to live in

A How much do you know about the planet Mars? Work with a partner and mark each statement *True* or *False*. Use your dictionary to help you understand the words in bold.

1. Scientists believe there was once a lot of water on the surface of Mars. That water is now **frozen** in the planet's **polar** regions.
2. Mars isn't a habitable planet for humans. It's too cold, and it has a very **thin** atmosphere.
3. There is less **gravity** on Mars than there is on Earth.
4. Mars is often called the "red planet" because its **soil** is red.

B Read the article's title and subtitle, and look at the image on page 67. How would you answer the questions in the subtitle? Discuss your ideas with a partner. Then read the article to check your ideas.

C How might humans transform Mars into a habitable planet? Match a time from the Thousand-Year Project with an event.

a. Every eighteen months
b. In the first one hundred years
c. By the year 200
d. By the year 600
e. By the year 1,000

1. _____ humans will be able to grow trees and other plants.
2. _____ humans will have started living in cities.
3. _____ an atmosphere starts to form as humans release CO_2 into the air.
4. _____ humans will travel to Mars; each new group will set up new buildings.
5. _____ water will have begun to flow and Mars's surface will have started to change.

Exploration on Mars

D Robert Zubrin gives two reasons for transforming Mars into a habitable planet. On a separate piece of paper, list the reasons and their benefits. Then compare answers with a partner.

Ask
Answer Do you think making Mars the new Earth is really feasible? Is it a good idea? Why or why not?

Making Mars the New Earth

What would it take to green[1] the red planet, and should we do it?

1   Could we transform Mars's frozen surface into something more friendly and Earthlike? And if we could, the question is: Should we? The first question has a clear answer: Yes, we probably could. Spacecraft exploring Mars have found evidence that the planet was warm in its youth and had rivers and large seas. Scientists believe that we could return Mars to this state by adding greenhouse gases like carbon dioxide into the planet's air. This would help create an atmosphere, which in turn would warm the planet, melt polar ice, and allow water to flow.

10   Transforming Mars into a habitable planet for humans could take centuries, but many supporters of the idea believe the effort would be worth it. Aerospace engineer Robert Zubrin, for example, believes that there are at least two good reasons to do it. The first is that going to Mars will challenge us, especially our youth. From this project, we could get millions of new scientists, doctors, inventors, and engineers. Zubrin also believes that if we open Mars to humanity, we will have a place for our species to grow and evolve, which will help to ensure humans' long-term survival. Zubrin anticipates that years from now there will be hundreds of colonies on Mars. Because

20   the gravity of Mars is less than on Earth, humans living there would eventually become lighter, taller, and slimmer. Earth people, by comparison, would appear a bit short and heavy. What we would have, says Zubrin, is species divergence.[2] In biology, he explains, a species is considered successful if it has many different types. Socially and culturally, humans would also evolve. Zubrin says Mars will be settled by different groups of people who want to live where the rules haven't been created yet. As a result, the inhabitants of Mars will likely develop a new way of life with unique languages, customs, literature, and technology.

30   Ultimately, manned missions to Mars would not only benefit people here on Earth, but also help to ensure humans' long-term survival. And for these reasons, say Zubrin and others, the journey and the expense would be worth it.

[1] **green** to make habitable for plant and animal life
[2] **divergence** separating; drawing apart

The THOUSAND-YEAR Project

Year 0: The project begins with a series of eighteen-month survey missions. Each crew making the six-month journey to Mars adds new housing and other buildings to the site.

Year 100: An atmosphere starts to form as humans add greenhouse gases like CO_2 into the planet's air.

Year 200: The temperature of the planet is now warmer. Rain starts to fall and water begins to flow. Mars's red soil begins to green very slightly.

Year 600: Small rivers and lakes have formed. There is now enough oxygen in the soil and atmosphere to grow flowers and plants.

Year 1,000: There are now a number of human colonies on Mars. Some people are living in cities. Though the planet is now warmer and greener, humans can still only go outside wearing breathing equipment. It will be thousands of years before there is enough oxygen outside for humans to move around without breathing equipment.

Writing
Make a Counterargument

A Read the first two paragraphs of this essay and then discuss Questions 1–3 with a partner.

Robert Zubrin feels that sending humans to Mars to transform it into a habitable planet is a good idea. Though he has some good reasons why we should do it, the disadvantages outweigh the benefits for three main reasons.

    The first drawback is the enormous risk and uncertainty of the project. Zubrin says that going to Mars will challenge us and help us produce millions of skilled workers. **However**, it's difficult to justify spending lots of money on a project where the chances of success are so uncertain. We know very little about living on Mars. Failure is actually quite feasible. If the mission is not successful, those millions of jobs will not come as expected. To truly challenge ourselves, we should start by using the money to research real problems we face right here on Earth, such as cancer or poverty.

1. Is the writer agreeing with or disagreeing with Robert Zubrin?
2. What reason does the writer give for her opinion?
3. Do you think she makes a good argument against Zubrin? Why or why not?

B Zubrin gives two more reasons why we should develop colonies on Mars. You want to argue against his ideas. Read items 2 and 3 below. Then match a drawback from the box with each of Zubrin's reasons or think of your own. Explain your reasons to a partner.

1. It will produce millions of new scientists, doctors, etc.
   Drawback: <u>the risk and uncertainty</u>
2. It will ensure humans' long-term survival.
   Drawback: _____
3. Humans will have the opportunity to create a new world with new rules.
   Drawback: _____

Possible Drawbacks
- We have problems to deal with on Earth first.
- Living in a place with no laws could be dangerous.
- Humans on Mars would face serious health risks.
- other: _____

C Write two more paragraphs for the essay in Exercise **A** on a separate piece of paper. Base these paragraphs on the drawbacks you listed in Exercise **B**.

1. First, read the Writing Strategy. Then for each paragraph, outline your ideas by doing the following: (1) state the drawback (*The second drawback is. . .*); (2) state Zubrin's point (*Zubrin says going to Mars will ensure. . .*); (3) offer your counterargument and clearly explain your reason (*However, . . .*).
2. Use your outline to write paragraphs 3 and 4.

Writing Strategy

Making a Counterargument
A counterargument, or rebuttal, argues against someone else's opinion, either because it is incorrect or because you have another point of view. A counterargument states:

- The opinion you disagree with: *Zubrin says that going to Mars will challenge us and help us produce millions of skilled workers.*
- Your opinion and reason for disagreeing: *However, it's difficult to justify spending lots of money on a project where the chances of success are so uncertain.*

Note that a rebuttal is often introduced using words like *however, yet,* and *that said.*

D Exchange papers with a partner, and read his or her paragraphs. Do you think your partner makes good counterarguments against Zubrin? Why or why not?

Speaking

A Read the questions below and think about your answers. You will need to support each of your responses with reasons and/or examples. Take some notes on a separate piece of paper.

1. In general, do you think space exploration is useful? Why or why not? Explain your answer.
2. Many people have said that given the chance, they would volunteer for a one-way journey to Mars to colonize the planet. If you were given that opportunity, would you do it? Why?
3. Every year, scientists discover more planets. Some say that it's feasible that by 2100 we will have made contact with other life forms. Does this make you feel hopeful or worried? Why?

B Work with a partner. Take turns answering the questions using your notes. You will have twenty minutes total. Continue until you have both answered each of the questions or time is up.

1. **Student A:** Choose one question (1–3) from Exercise **A** and answer it. Talk for one minute.

   Student B: When your partner is finished, answer these questions and share your feedback with Student A:

   - Did Student A keep talking without stopping or hesitating a lot?
   - Did Student A explain his or her ideas in detail and make sense when he/she talked?

2. Switch roles and repeat steps 1 and 2 until all questions are answered.

C Share your answers with the class. Which were the most common? Do the results surprise you?

Video

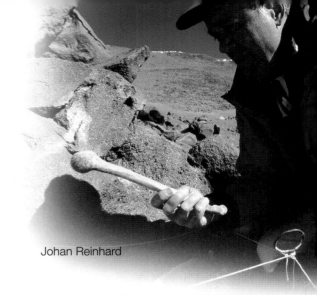

Johan Reinhard

> **inspire** to encourage or make someone want to do something

A Read the information about three National Geographic explorers. Have you ever heard of these people? What do these three explorers have in common? Tell a partner.

ALEXANDRA COUSTEAU

Environmental advocate (and granddaughter of Jacques Cousteau) who raises awareness about global water issues and inspires people to protect the planet's waters

JOHAN REINHARD

Anthropologist who has done extensive field research in the Andes and Himalayas investigating the cultural practices of mountain people

SYLVIA EARLE

Oceanographer who has led numerous underwater expeditions around the world, researching marine ecosystems and advocating for the environment

B Read these questions. Next, watch the video of Alexandra Cousteau and write the numbers (1–2) of the questions she answers. Then watch the video of Johan Reinhard and Sylvia Earle and do the same.

1. When you were young, what inspired your interest in exploration?
2. What is the most exciting part of your job?

(Segment 1): Alexandra Cousteau _____   **(Segment 2):** Johan Reinhard _____

(Segment 3): Sylvia Earle _____

C Read the excerpts from the video below. Then watch the video again and paraphrase each underlined word or expression with a partner. Write on a separate piece of paper and use your dictionary to help you.

1. **Cousteau:** Every new place is always a <u>revelation</u>.
2. **Reinhard:** Probably the things that most excited me for discoveries weren't so much the mummies <u>per se</u>, but . . .

3. **Earle:** It's finding, not just new things, but new ideas to begin to <u>connect the dots</u>.

D Join another pair and choose one side of the following question: *Which kind of exploration is more important: ocean exploration or archeological exploration?* Pairs should not choose the same side of the debate. Carefully plan your argument and then debate your position against the other pair.

Sylvia Earle

Expanding Your Fluency

It is the year 2200. You and your classmates are colonists on your way to Mars. Though humans have been going to Mars for several years, the life you'll lead will still be fairly primitive:

- You'll be living in a small house, which you will share with four other people. You'll be spending a lot of time inside, as it will only be about 32°F (0°C) outside during the day.
- You won't have running water, and personal electricity use will be limited to one hour a day. Entertainment that you took for granted on Earth (movies, music, games) won't exist on Mars.
- Once a year, you will receive food, clothing, and medical supplies from Earth, but for the most part, you will need to grow all of your own food and repair everything you own.

Other facts:

- There are already fifty other small colonies on the planet populated by adults and children. Some are friendly and open, while others are closed and hostile to outsiders.
- People speak different languages.
- Once a month, colonies trade goods and interact with each other at indoor marketplaces.

 Read the information above. Then get into a group of five people and do the following:

1. Each person should choose a role: architect, environmentalist, interpreter, nurse, engineer android, or another role of your choosing. On your own, think about these questions:

   - What skills or talents do you bring to the group?
   - How will you be able to improve the quality of life for yourself and your fellow colonists?
   - What job(s) will you be able to do?

2. Explain your answers to your partners; they will ask you questions to learn more.

3. Once on Mars, your group discovers that you have only enough resources to support <u>four</u> colonists. Because of this, one of you must leave the colony. Each person in the group will have one minute to explain why he or she should stay and why the others should leave.

4. Which person would you vote out of the colony? State who you chose to "vote off" and explain your reasons. The person who receives the most votes must go.

Check What You Know

Rank how well you can perform these outcomes on a scale of 1–5 (5 being the best).

_____ make predictions using different future forms

_____ identify key words used to explain reasons

_____ describe skills needed to achieve future goals

_____ develop and write a counterargument

7 Live and Learn

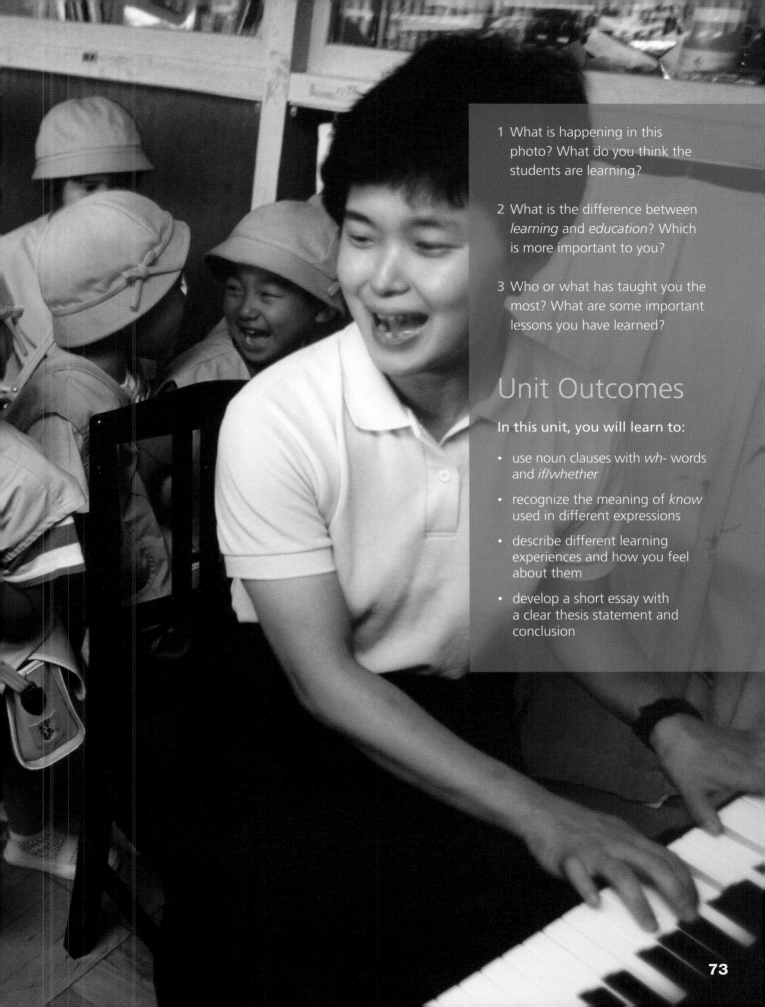

1 What is happening in this photo? What do you think the students are learning?

2 What is the difference between *learning* and *education*? Which is more important to you?

3 Who or what has taught you the most? What are some important lessons you have learned?

Unit Outcomes

In this unit, you will learn to:

• use noun clauses with *wh-* words and *if/whether*

• recognize the meaning of *know* used in different expressions

• describe different learning experiences and how you feel about them

• develop a short essay with a clear thesis statement and conclusion

Vocabulary

accomplish to achieve something or succeed at doing something

aptitude ability to learn a type of work or activity quickly and do it well

common sense a person's natural ability to make good judgments and behave sensibly

excel to be very good at doing something

instinct the natural tendency of a person to behave or react a certain way

intellectual someone who studies a lot and thinks about complicated ideas

master someone who is extremely skilled at a particular activity

outcome a result or effect of an action or situation

strategy planning the best way to gain advantage or achieve success

street smarts the quick-thinking ability to handle difficult or dangerous situations, especially in big cities

work out to find a solution to a problem

Garry Kasparov versus Deep Blue

A Look at the nouns in the word bank. Which ones describe an intelligence that you are born with? Which describe an intelligence that is learned? Discuss with a partner.

B Complete this profile of Garry Kasparov with the correct words. When you're done, tell a partner who he is and what makes him such an exceptional chess player.

Scientists, computer experts, and other (1) **intellectuals / masters** have often wondered: Who is smarter, man or machine? Garry Kasparov, a Russian chess (2) **intellectual / master** who has a natural (3) **instinct / strategy** for the game, attempted to answer that question. His (4) **aptitude / outcome** for chess, a game of (5) **street smarts / strategy**, was discovered at a young age. As a teenager he (6) **excelled / worked out** at the game, and by age twenty-two he had become the youngest World Champion ever.

In chess, players have to (7) **accomplish / work out** solutions for each move they make; they have to plan several moves ahead using (8) **outcomes / common sense** and logic. Garry's outstanding ability to do this quickly helped him become one of the greatest chess players in history.

In 1996, Garry played against a computer named Deep Blue, which was able to analyze fifty billion moves in three minutes. No one could have possibly predicted the (9) **outcome / strategy**. To everyone's surprise, Garry (10) **accomplished / worked out** his goal of beating Deep Blue.

C With a partner, discuss the situations below. Would a computer or a person be better at them? Why?

I think a person would be better at giving directions. A computer might know the shortest route, but it might send you to a dangerous part of town!

1. giving directions to a tourist
2. taking a timed math test

3. picking out a gift for someone
4. playing video games

5. writing a hit song
6. designing a house

Ask

Answer Who do you think is smarter, man or machine? Why?

Grammar

A On a separate piece of paper, combine these sentences with the words in parentheses to make noun clauses.

1. Is our class meeting today? I have no idea. (whether)
2. Is Mr. Jones teaching chemistry? I'm not sure. (if)
3. Should I graduate early? I'll consider it. (whether)
4. Did they like the class? I don't know. (if)

Noun Clauses with *Wh-* Words and *If/Whether*

wh- clauses	Combine a *wh-* question and a statement. Change the question to statement word order.
	She taught sixty students in one class. How does she do it? → *I don't know how she teaches sixty students in one class.*
***if/whether* clauses**	Combine a *yes/no* question and a statement.
	Did he pass the exam? I wonder. → *I wonder if/whether he passed the exam (or not).*
	If and *whether* are often interchangeable, but they are not quite the same. Use *if* when the noun clause outlines one condition. Use *whether (or not)* when the noun clause states alternative possibilities, whether explicitly stated or implied.
	*Let Anne know **if** Jack is coming.* (Anne only needs to be contacted if Jack is coming.)
	*Let Anne know **whether** Jack is coming.* (Anne needs to be contacted whether he comes or not.)

B Take turns choosing a question from the list and trying to answer it.

- If you're not sure of the answer, use one of the expressions in the box to answer with a *wh-* clause or *if/whether* clause. Ask your group members for their opinions.
- If you know the answer or have an opinion, try to give your answer with a noun clause beginning with *that*.

certain	forget	have no idea	know	remember	see	sure	tell	understand	wonder

1. Is college tuition expensive?
2. Are there good universities in your country?
3. How many students study abroad every year?
4. Does a good education guarantee a good job?
5. What is the minimum TOEFL score you need?
6. Do straight-A students have street smarts?
7. What is a good way to master English?
8. Should high school graduates take time off?
9. What's the most efficient way to study?
10. Is it possible to learn a foreign language fluently as an adult?

> I don't know if a good education guarantees a good job or not. What do you think?

> I believe that a good education helps a lot, but I don't know whether it will guarantee you a good job.

Listening

A Read the information in the box. Then discuss the questions with a partner.

> Some students take a year-long break from school (often right after high school graduation, but before entering college) to travel, study something, or work. Some students choose to spend this year in another country.

- Why do you think some students take a year off?
- What are the advantages and disadvantages of taking a year off after high school?

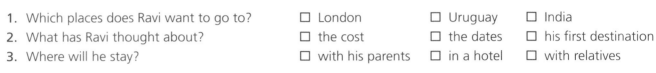

The Gherkin, a building [in] London's financial distric[t]

B Listen to a conversation between Ravi and Sophie. Choose the best answer(s) for each question.

1. Which places does Ravi want to go to?   ☐ London   ☐ Uruguay   ☐ India
2. What has Ravi thought about?   ☐ the cost   ☐ the dates   ☐ his first destination
3. Where will he stay?   ☐ with his parents   ☐ in a hotel   ☐ with relatives

C What can you infer about Ravi and Sophie? Listen again and mark each statement *True* or *False* and explain your answers to a partner.

1. Ravi is going to study medicine.
2. Ravi excelled in his studies.
3. He's financially responsible.
4. He grew up in India.
5. Sophie has taken a year off before.
6. Ravi has talked to his dad already.

D Read the Listening Strategy. Then listen and match each expression with *know* to its meaning, according to the context of the conversation.

1. *I know, I know.*
2. *As far as I know . . .*
3. *You know what I'm saying?*
4. *. . .who knows?*
5. *. . .you never know.*

a. Do you understand what I mean?
b. I'm not sure; I don't know.
c. I agree with you.
d. Anything is possible.
e. I don't have all the information, but I think (a situation) is true.

Listening Strategy   **Understanding t[he] Meaning of *Kno[w]***
The word *know* is used in a number of common expressions in English to show agreement, to express certainty or uncertainty, to check for understan[d] and to talk about possibility. Learni[ng] these expressions will help you foll[ow] cues that indicate the speaker's atti[tude] towards the topic.

Ask

Answer   If you could take a year off right now, how would you spend the time?

PRONUNCIATION In collocations such as *have to, ought to,* and *going to*, the *to* i[s] unstressed. The vowel sound gets reduced to a sound called *schwa*. Listen for these collocations in the conversation. Then pract[ice] saying them with schwa. For more on redu[cing] to schwa, see p. 146.

Connections

A Look at the list of skills and the occupations. Discuss the questions below with a partner.

> a. academic intelligence / book smarts
> b. artistic talent
> c. common sense
> d. interpersonal skills
> e. logical thinking
> f. street smarts
> g. visual aptitude
> h. physical strength / agility
> i. other: _____

CEO _____   interior designer _____

journalist _____   police officer _____

1. Match the skills with the occupations. Which skills would people in those jobs need the most? Why?
2. What challenges would a person lacking these skills face?
3. In which skills do you tend to excel?

> I don't know whether or not a police officer needs book smarts, but he or she would definitely need to have street smarts. A police officer also needs . . .

B Get into a group of four people. Read the instructions to play the game below.

Do you have what it takes? is an expression meaning "Do you have the background or skills necessary to do something?"

1. Write each occupation in Exercise **A** on a slip of paper. Each person in the group should also write one more occupation. Shuffle and lay all of the papers face down on the desk.
2. One person begins by turning over a slip of paper. The player will have one minute to convince the others that he / she could do that job. The other players should ask the speaker follow-up questions.
3. When time is up, the other players should discuss and decide whether or not the speaker has what it takes to do the job. If the speaker convinced them, he / she gets one point. If the speaker's argument was unconvincing, he / she gets no points.
4. Return the paper to the desk. It is then the next person's turn. Play until each person has had a chance to talk about each occupation. The winner is the person with the most points.

> She says she has street smarts and common sense, but I'm not sure if she'd really make a good police officer. She's not very responsible.

Video

narrow down to remove items from a list so
   that only the most important ones remain
nonsense silly or untrue
objective neutral; based only on facts

A Discuss the questions with a partner.

1. What are the top three universities in your
   country? Why are they considered the best?
2. Which criteria would you use to choose a
   university? Why?

   • cost of tuition

   • location

   • overall reputation

   • student-to-teacher ratio

   • reputations of departments

   • other: _____

I would go to the university with the best reputation,
whether it was expensive or not!

Oxford (pictured) and Cambridge are two of the most
prestigious universities in the world, but there are
distinctions between the two. Oxford is considered
stronger in humanities, while Cambridge has a
reputation for excellence in the sciences.

B Read the information in the box below. Then watch segment 1. Does each person think university rankings
   are useful or not useful? Mark the correct answer, and write the key words that helped you choose it.

> The rankings of the world's best universities influence where students decide to apply and enroll. However,
> some people question whether these rankings are useful or not. UNESCO, the United Nations Educational,
> Scientific and Cultural Organization, asked some students and administrators to give their opinions.

1. Woman from Thailand   useful / not useful   key words: _____
2. Woman from Venezuela   useful / not useful   key words: _____
3. Man from Sweden   useful / not useful   key words: _____
4. Man from Cameroon   useful / not useful   key words: _____
5. Man from the Netherlands   useful / not useful   key words: _____

C Read the question and then watch segment 2. How does each woman respond? Mark the correct answer.

Could an organization like UNESCO help students decide which university is best?

1. Woman from Trinidad and Tobago   yes / no   2. Woman from Lebanon   yes / no

D Watch segment 2 again and take notes. Then
   summarize for a partner what each woman said.

Ask
Answer   Do you think that university
         rankings are helpful or not?

78   Unit 7

Speaking

A With a partner, discuss the questions below.

1. Do you think academic success is necessary to be successful in life?
2. British Prime Minister Winston Churchill, one of the most important world leaders of the twentieth century, once said, "My education was only interrupted by my schooling." What do you think he meant by that?

B The list below names different sources of learning. Read the list and give an example of what you can learn or have learned from each.

Source	Learning potential
good teacher	
parent	
friends	
travel	
sports or other activity	
job	You can learn the importance of being on time from a job.
books	
your idea: _____	

C In pairs, share your thoughts on the list from Exercise **B**.

> I think a good teacher is really important because he or she can inspire you and can give you confidence. For example, I always hated languages until I had English with Mr. Morgan two years ago . . .

Reading

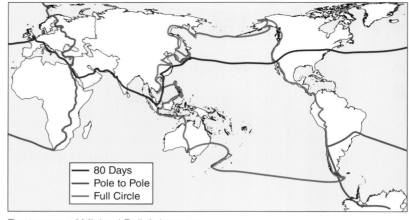

Route map of Michael Palin's journeys

A Read the quotations in the box with the article. Then read items 1–4 below, which are paraphrases of the quotations, and match them to their source. Which opinion(s) do you agree with? Why? What do you think these travelers may have learned from their travels? Tell a partner.

1. Traveling teaches you to appreciate home.
2. You can learn something new from each place you travel to.
3. Travel helps people from different backgrounds to know one another.
4. Travel helps you gain a greater appreciation for humanity.

a. St. Augustine
b. Moorish proverb
c. Lin Yutang
d. Mark Twain

B Read the article about Michael Palin. On another piece of paper, list the trips he has completed and a brief description of each.

C Reread the article's last paragraph and, in your own words, explain to a partner why Palin's documentaries are so popular with viewers.

D Read the Reading Strategy. Which words does the writer substitute for the word *trip* in the article? Underline as many synonyms as you can find in the article. Then compare ideas with a partner.

Reading Strategy

Recognizing Synonyms
Writers will often use synonyms for common words in their writing. For example, instead of repeating the expression "the <u>story</u> of his life," the writer may substitute the word *story* with alternatives such as *tale, record, diary,* or *account.*

Ask
Answer   What kind of life lessons can you learn by traveling, both in your own country and abroad?

The Sahara Desert

The World Is Our Classroom

Traveler profile: *Michael Palin*

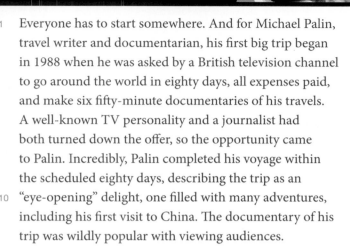

Notable and Quotable

"Travel is fatal to prejudice, bigotry, and narrow-mindedness."
—*Mark Twain*

"The world is a book and those who do not travel read only one page."
—*St. Augustine*

"He who does not travel does not know the value of men."
—*Moorish proverb*

"No one realizes how beautiful it is to travel until he comes home and rests his head on his old, familiar pillow."
—*Lin Yutang*

1 Everyone has to start somewhere. And for Michael Palin, travel writer and documentarian, his first big trip began in 1988 when he was asked by a British television channel to go around the world in eighty days, all expenses paid, and make six fifty-minute documentaries of his travels. A well-known TV personality and a journalist had both turned down the offer, so the opportunity came to Palin. Incredibly, Palin completed his voyage within the scheduled eighty days, describing the trip as an
10 "eye-opening" delight, one filled with many adventures, including his first visit to China. The documentary of his trip was wildly popular with viewing audiences.

His first long journey had been satisfying, so when Palin was asked to go on another, he readily agreed. During his first trip, Palin had traveled around the world horizontally. Now the plan was for him to do it vertically by going from the North Pole to the South Pole. For the "Pole to Pole" trek, Palin began near the Arctic Circle. From there he traveled south through Europe, across
20 the Mediterranean, through Africa, ultimately reaching his final destination of Antarctica five months later. The journey was so challenging that, by the end of it, he vowed[1] never to do another travel documentary again.

But after seeing so many amazing people and places, he couldn't stop. His next expedition, called "Full Circle," documented his trip around the countries surrounding the Pacific Ocean. It was the longest, most ambitious, and most exhausting of all his travels. He covered 50,000 miles (80,000 km), traveled through
30 seventeen countries, and filmed for ten months. In later outings he crossed the Sahara, enduring the blinding sandstorms and punishing heat that the desert is known

for. He also explored and filmed in the Himalayas, experiencing the anxiety and physical demands of working at high altitude.

In total, Palin has made seven major international trips that he has recorded both visually and in writing. However, he has also gone on smaller, more personal treks, such as "From Derry to Kerry." Travelling across
40 Ireland, Palin went in search of his family's own story, tracing his great-grandmother's roots, and learning about the journey his own family took from Ireland to the United States in the 1800s.

Millions enjoy Palin's films and books. What exactly is it that draws people to his stories of restless wanderings? One of the main things is Palin's remarkable energy. For many of his journeys he is on the road for months at a time, traveling to each destination by car, train, or bus, very rarely going anywhere by plane. The challenge is
50 hard to believe but fun to watch. Second, because Palin spends such a long time in each place, viewers are able to get a more realistic, less stereotyped[2] view of what life in each location is really like. And finally, Palin is a master storyteller—people enjoy his work because each of his accounts are so rich and complex. Viewers feel as though they are participating in the adventure with him. For his next trip, Michael Palin will be exploring Brazil . . . and his fans can't wait to learn all about it!

[1] **vow** to make a promise to oneself or another
[2] **stereotype** the general idea that one has about an entire group of people

Writing

Describe a Life Lesson

A Read the personal essay below. What happened to the writer?

Was it a positive or negative experience? What did she learn from it? Tell a partner.

One of the most important lessons I ever learned didn't come from a textbook or take place in a classroom. When I was fourteen, I was diagnosed with diabetes.[1] <u>Though the experience was difficult, it taught me some valuable life lessons that have really helped me.</u>

People often say that teenagers are able to have fun and not take life too seriously, but that's not always true. In my case, because of my illness, I always had to be very responsible. This was hard for me, both physically and socially. The first year after my diagnosis, I was hospitalized twice. In school, some people didn't understand why I had to be careful about what I ate or why I had to give myself shots. Some of my classmates even made fun of me. Those were tough times, but luckily I had my mom by my side. Whenever I fell down, she encouraged me to focus on the good things—my friends, my family, my education, and my goals. I didn't know if I could do it, but I tried. In time, I learned how to live with my illness. I also worked hard and excelled in school. I even tried out for and got a big part in the school play. Before I got sick, I wouldn't have been brave enough to do that.

There's a saying that "experience is the best teacher" and I believe it. My illness taught me that sometimes a bad situation can motivate you to do your best and even try new things. It also taught me to recognize the important things in life and to really appreciate them. Even now, when I am upset about something, I remind myself that life is good and that I am very lucky. <u>Living with diabetes hasn't been easy, but the experience has taught me some important life lessons—ones that I continue to benefit from every day.</u>

 TIP You can use a saying or quote to illustrate or reinforce a point, as the writer does at the start of the third paragraph.

[1] **diabetes** an illness in which someone can't process sugar normally

> **Writing Strategy**
>
> **Writing a Thesis Statement and a Conclusion**
> A **thesis statement** (see the first underlined sentence) tells readers what the essay is generally going to be about. It typically comes at the end of the first paragraph of an essay.
> A **concluding sentence** (see the second underlined sentence) brings the piece of writing to a close. One of the most common ways of writing a concluding sentence is to restate the thesis statement. Write this sentence in a different way—try not to repeat the exact same words as the thesis statement.

B Read the Writing Strategy. Then think about a positive or negative experience that taught you an important life lesson. Outline your ideas on a separate piece of paper.

Paragraph 1: Briefly introduce the experience: What was it and when did it happen? Include a thesis statement at the end of the paragraph.

Paragraph 2: Describe the experience in detail: What happened exactly?

Paragraph 3: Explain what you learned: What did the experience teach you and how did it impact your life? Close with a concluding sentence that summarizes the experience.

C Write your essay using your notes from Exercise **B**.

D Exchange papers with a partner. Does your partner's essay have three paragraphs that answer the questions in Exercise **B**? Does the essay have a clear thesis statement and conclusion? What could your partner do to improve his or her essay?

Expanding Your Fluency

A Take four small pieces of paper. Write your response to each item below on a separate piece of paper (one item on each paper). Write the corresponding item number (1–4) on the other side of the paper.

1. Write your full name, birthday, favorite color, and a piece of contact information (for example, your phone number or e-mail address).
2. List a strategy you use to study for an English test.
3. Write one of your personal goals and list the steps you plan to take to accomplish it.
4. Write the name of a book or movie that really affected you. Also list the main character's name. In a sentence or two, explain what you liked about or learned from the book or movie.

B Exchange papers with a partner. Try to memorize all of the information on the papers. You will have three minutes to do this.

C Return the papers back to your partner and see how much you remember. Take turns repeating the information from each piece of paper. Who has the most points at the end?

- Score 2 points per paper if you remember all the information exactly.
- Score 1 point per paper if you remember some of the information.
- Score 0 points per paper if you can't remember any information.

> I know that Mia read *The Hunger Games,* but I don't remember whether the main character's name was Katniss or Kaynee . . .

Check What You Know

Rank how well you can perform these outcomes on a scale of 1–5 (5 being the best).

_____ use noun clauses with *wh-* words and *if/whether*

_____ recognize the meaning of *know* used in different expressions

_____ describe different learning experiences and how you feel about them

_____ develop a short essay with a clear thesis statement and conclusion

8 The Cult of Celebrity

1 This man was hiding behind a tree. Why would he do that? What kind of job do you think he has?

2 Which celebrity would you cancel all your plans for the opportunity to see? Why did you choose that person?

3 Think of a celebrity whom you'd like to meet. What are three questions you'd like to ask him or her?

Unit Outcomes

In this unit, you will learn to:

• use reported speech to report questions

• use key words to summarize a writer's ideas

• consider the advantages and disadvantages of fame

• write an opinion piece that is supported by facts

Vocabulary

appealing pleasing and attractive

background the kind of work, life, and family experience you have

celebrated famous and much admired

cultivate to try hard to develop something or make it stronger

exposure public attention that a person, company, or product receives

invest to put time or money into something because you think it will be beneficial

notorious to be famous for something bad

paparazzi photographers who follow celebrities, photograph them, and sell the pictures

remarkable unusual or special in a way that gets attention

renowned to be famous for something good

socialite a person who attends many fashionable upper-class social events

A Read about these three famous people. What did they do to become famous? Discuss with a partner. Then read the article and choose the correct words.

Paris Hilton didn't have any (1) **background / socialite** in acting, but she knew that she could get on TV by starring in her own reality TV show. "The Simple Life" followed two wealthy (2) **socialites / paparazzi** (Paris and her friend Nicole) as they worked as maids, farmhands, and fast food restaurant employees. Soon everyone was talking about Paris, who, unlike other celebrities, has (3) **cultivated / invested** a relationship with the (4) **exposure / paparazzi**.

How did Paris Hilton become a celebrity?

Steve Jobs was the former CEO of Apple Inc. Along with company cofounder Steve Wozniak, he created one of the first commercially successful personal computers. He was (5) **renowned / cultivated** for his (6) **notorious / remarkable** business sense. This shows in successful products such as the iPad and iPhone, which consumers like because of their (7) **appealing / renowned** design and simplicity. Not afraid to (8) **cultivate / invest** time and money into new ideas, Jobs was often called a "design perfectionist." His path to fame involved having good ideas and implementing them before anyone else.

Construction worker Wesley Autrey was waiting for the subway when he saw a young man have a seizure and fall onto the tracks. Autrey jumped down and protected the young man from an oncoming train. Since then, he has become a (9) **celebrated / notorious** local hero and received lots of media (10) **background / exposure** (interviews on news programs and talk shows). At a time when we hear so much in the news about (11) **remarkable / notorious** criminals, this story about an ordinary man who acted heroically is truly heartwarming.

B Read this list of ways to become famous. Discuss the questions with a partner.

What are the advantages and disadvantages of each method? Which would be hardest to do? Why? Which of these methods would you try?

- invent something that everyone wants
- star on a reality TV show
- do the right thing and become a hero
- befriend a famous person
- get attention for being bad at something
- win a contest on TV
- other: _____

Grammar

A Choose the best answers.

1. Tom asked me, "Who is your favorite celebrity?" He asked me _____.
   a. who was my favorite celebrity   b. who my favorite celebrity was

2. Jen asked me, "Do you want to be famous someday?" She asked me _____.
   a. that I wanted to be famous someday   b. if I wanted to be famous someday

B Look at the photo and read the information in the grammar chart. In reported questions, what changes do you notice to the verb tenses and pronouns?

Reported Questions	
Quoted Speech	**Reported Speech**
Yes/no questions: Are you going to win an award?	❶ They asked him **if he was going to win an award**. They asked him **whether (or not) he was going to win an award**. They asked him **whether he was going to win an award (or not)**.
Are you getting tired of the paparazzi?	She asked him **if he was getting tired of the paparazzi**.
***Wh-* questions:** Who are you here with?	❷ He asked him **who he was there with**.
Where are you going?	They wanted to know **where he was going**.
❶ Notice how the verb forms change (backshift) in reported questions. ❷ Notice the shift from *here* to *there*. ❸ You can use the expression *want to know* in place of *ask*.	

C Imagine you are a celebrity. You are telling a friend about the questions you were asked last week. Complete the sentences, using reported speech.

Yes/no questions	*Wh-* questions
1. Can I have your autograph?	5. What designer are you wearing?
2. Do you like it here?	6. Who has inspired you most in your career?
3. Are all the rumors true?	7. What is your new movie about?
4. your idea: _____	8. your idea: _____

1. Many fans asked _____.
2. A stranger asked _____.
3. The paparazzi wanted to know _____.
4. _____.
5. On the red carpet they wanted to know _____.
6. An interviewer wanted to know _____.
7. Everyone asked _____.
8. _____.

D Which questions in Exercise **C** wouldn't bother you? Which questions would you hate to answer and why? Discuss your answers with a partner.

Listening

> **flock to** to go to a particular place or event because it's interesting, usually in large numbers
>
> **transition** the process in which something changes from one state to another

A Look at the photo of Mary Pickford, an early actress who paid the price for her fame. Who do you think she was? What do you think might have happened to her? Discuss with a partner.

B Listen to a conversation about the actress Mary Pickford. Mark each statement *True* or *False*. Then check your answers with a partner and explain your choices.

Mary Pickford, "America's Sweetheart"

	True	False
1. Mary Pickford's family was wealthy.	☐	☐
2. People liked to see Mary Pickford in the movies and read about her.	☐	☐
3. She was called "America's Sweetheart" because she was a hard worker.	☐	☐
4. As Mary Pickford grew older, the public adored her new roles.	☐	☐
5. It was difficult for Mary Pickford to move from silent to talking films.	☐	☐

C Listen again and complete the sentences in the timeline.

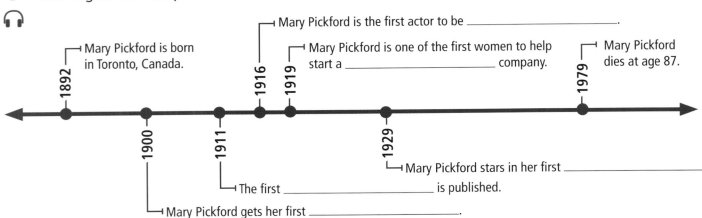

1892 Mary Pickford is born in Toronto, Canada.

1916 Mary Pickford is the first actor to be _____.

1919 Mary Pickford is one of the first women to help start a _____ company.

1979 Mary Pickford dies at age 87.

1900 Mary Pickford gets her first _____.

1911 The first _____ is published.

1929 Mary Pickford stars in her first _____.

> **Ask**
>
> **Answer** Actors are pressured to look young and beautiful, even as they grow older. What effect does this pressure have on them? What effect does constantly seeing "perfect looking" actors have on audiences?

Connections

A You are going to role-play an encounter between an actor and a paparazzo. Follow these steps.

1. Complete the information about the actor below. Then choose the role (actor or paparazzo) you want to play.
2. Read the first part of the conversation below.
3. Write the rest of the conversation on a separate sheet of paper. Include three more questions for the paparazzo to ask.
4. At the end of the conversation, the actor should get frustrated and threaten to call the police. The paparazzo should then leave.
5. Practice your conversation a couple of times.

Roles

Student A (actor)
You were recently voted "The Year's Most Appealing Actor." You have a background in _____ and are known for your work as _____ . You are popular, but also notorious for _____ .

Student B (paparazzo)
Your company has invested a lot of time and money in trying to photograph and interview this actor. As a paparazzo, you are renowned for "never giving up." Your strategy is to "sweet talk" the actor—give compliments to get what you want!

> The singular form of **paparazzi** is **paparazzo**.

Conversation

Paparazzo: Excuse me, aren't you _____ ?
Actor: Yes, I am.
Paparazzo: Well, can I take your picture please?
Actor: No, no! Please go away.
Paparazzo: Could you just answer a couple questions for me?
Actor: I'm sorry. Not today. I've had too much bad exposure lately.
Paparazzo: Please! You are one of the most remarkable actors. I promise that I'll only ask you a few questions.
Actor: Well, maybe if it's just a few . . .

B Student A from Exercise **A** should now find a Student B from a different pair. Role-play a conversation between the actor and a police officer. Student A will still play the role of the actor, and Student B will now be a police officer.

So, what did he say?

He asked if he could take my picture.

And what did you say?

I told him to please go away.

And then what happened?

He wanted to know if . . .

Roles

Student A (celebrity actor)
You were really annoyed by the paparazzo's questions and want to make a complaint. Talk to a police officer and answer some questions. Use reported speech when necessary.

Student B (police officer)
Ask the actor what happened. Take notes so you can make a report about it later.

Reading

A Read the information in the box. Can you name any celebrity endorsements? Which ones are most memorable? Why? Discuss with a partner.

> **To endorse** means "to make a public statement of approval or support for something or someone." A **celebrity endorsement** happens when a famous person appears in an advertisement saying they use a certain product.

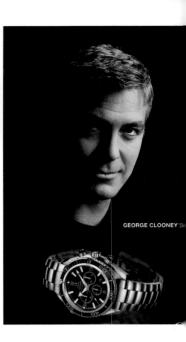

GEORGE CLOONEY Si

B Find the words below in the interview on page 91. Choose the option (*a.* or *b.*) that is most similar in meaning to the word used in the interview.

1. adore (paragraph 1)	a. love	b. hate
2. exorbitant (paragraph 2)	a. dirt cheap	b. outrageously expensive
3. pitching (paragraph 2)	a. buying	b. promoting
4. doable (paragraph 4)	a. possible (to do)	b. impossible (to do)
5. nominal (paragraph 5)	a. small (amount)	b. large (amount)
6. merchandise (paragraph 6)	a. advertisements	b. products
7. personable (paragraph 6)	a. efficient (in service)	b. pleasant (in character)

C Skim the interview on page 91. Then match each of the interviewer's questions below with one of Ben's answers. One has already been done for you.

<u>Paragraph 2</u>   OK, let's say, for example, that I work for a large company and have a lot of money to spend. How hard is it to get a celebrity to endorse my product?

_____ Can you give me an example of a company that received a big endorsement without paying for it?

_____ But what if my company is a small start-up and can't afford to pay celebrities the large amounts of money that big corporations do?

_____ You've talked about two extremes: spending a lot of money on endorsements or getting them for free. What if I have a limited budget for an endorsement?

_____ Really? You can get an endorsement for free? I wonder if that's realistic.

_____ What exactly are celebrity endorsements?

Reading Strategy   **Summarizing the Writer's Ideas**   You can better understand the writer's ideas by writing a one-sentence summary of each paragraph. (This will help you remember what you've read and help you explain the piece to others.) When writing your summary, pick out key words from each paragraph that you want to reuse. For example, in the first paragraph you might choose the words *celebrity, endorse, consumer,* and *buy.* Then use those words in your summary: *Once a **celebrity** has **endorsed** a product, the idea is that **consumers** will want to **buy** and use it too.*

D How does Ben answer the interviewer's questions? On a separate piece of paper list the key words for each answer. Then, using those key words, write a one-sentence summary for each of Ben's replies.

Ask

Answer   Do you think celebrity endorsements work? Why or why not?

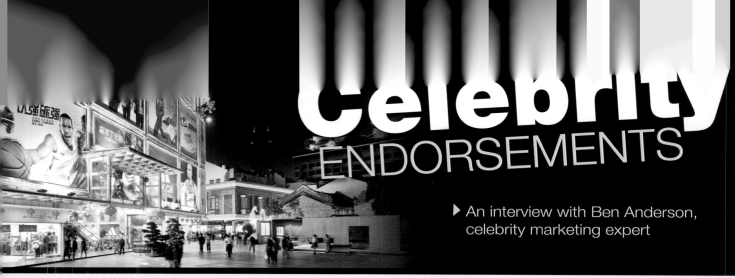

Celebrity ENDORSEMENTS

▶ An interview with Ben Anderson, celebrity marketing expert

1.

Interviewer: _____

Ben: The idea behind celebrity endorsements is pretty simple. The public adores their celebrities. They love to read about them online and watch their TV shows, athletic performances, and movies. When those celebrities wear a certain piece of clothing or eat a particular food, and then talk about it, the product then gets a lot of attention. Once a celebrity has endorsed a product, such as a weight loss plan or a new car, people start asking where they can buy it. The idea is that consumers will want to buy and use the very same products that they think celebrities buy and use themselves.

2.

Interviewer: <u>OK, let's say, for example, that I work for a large company and have a lot of money to spend. How hard is it to get a celebrity to endorse my product?</u>

Ben: If you have a lot of money, and many big corporations do, getting a celebrity endorsement is not so difficult. It's true that the most popular celebrities charge an exorbitant fee for endorsements, but if you have a large budget it's not a problem. You simply ask the celebrity if they will work with you. If they say "yes," you then draw up a contract and get to work. Did you know that as many as one-fifth of all ads feature well-known celebrities pitching products? A big company may spend as much as half a billion dollars a year on endorsements.

3.

Interviewer: _____

Ben: Well, it's definitely more challenging for smaller companies to get endorsements, but it's not impossible. The most important thing is to get your product into the hands of the celebrity somehow, so that people can see him or her using it. If you are creative, you can sometimes avoid spending any money at all!

4.

Interviewer: _____

Ben: It's totally doable. One way is by participating in a major event, such as an awards show. On those occasions, a variety of products are packaged in gift bags and then given out for free to celebrities who attend the event. Get your product into those gift bags and there's a chance a famous person may try your product, like it, and later endorse it!

5.

Interviewer: _____

Ben: If you have a limited budget to work with, you'll just have to work with lesser-known stars. You won't be able to afford Lionel Messi or Adele, but that's OK. In this situation, what you will do is pay your star a nominal fee and give them free merchandise. The celebrity then models with your product in a photo. You post the photo on your company's Website so that everyone can see the celebrity using your product.

6.

Interviewer: _____

Ben: Sure. There was this one small start-up that made stylish shoes for people with large feet. One day a very tall customer wandered into their store and asked the staff if they could help him. He couldn't find shoes that would fit him. The man left the store that day a very satisfied customer with three new pairs of shoes. It turns out that he was the brother of a popular professional basketball player. Soon most of the team was regularly shopping there, while also messaging their fans about how wonderful the store was. The merchandise started to fly off the shelves, all because the initial customer had received a good product with personable service.

Speaking

A Look at the products below. Answer the questions with a partner.

- What are these products and who do you think they would appeal to?
- Imagine you work for an advertising company and need to get a celebrity endorsement for one of these products. Which product would you choose and why?

B You and your partner are going to choose a celebrity to endorse your product. Consider the qualities listed below as you discuss and decide which celebrity would best represent your product.

sense of style	public behavior (role model)
attractiveness	personal background
personality	past success
relationship with fans	potential for sales

C Join another pair and present your ideas. After you listen, answer these questions.

- What do you think of the other pair's choice of celebrity? What are the benefits and drawbacks of having that celebrity endorse the product?
- Would you buy the product? Why or why not?

> **PRONUNCIATION** The sentence *He would be the **perfect** celebrity to promote that product.* can be said sincerely or sarcastically depending on your intonation. For more on intonation to show sarcasm and irony, see p. 147.

Ask

Answer Has a celebrity endorsement ever caused you to buy a product?

Video

commemorative officially remembering a famous person or major event

icon an important symbol of something

status an accepted or official position

A Read and answer the questions about the photo.

Kate Middleton, the Duchess of Cambridge, lives her life in the public eye. What do you know about her? What are some of the challenges of always being in the spotlight?

B Watch the video and then choose the best answer for each item.

1. What happened when Kate wore a designer coat on a visit to Ireland?
   a. The price of the coat doubled overnight.
   b. The coat quickly sold out.

2. What happened when Kate started wearing different hats?
   a. She became a big celebrity all over the world.
   b. Other celebrities started wearing hats too.

3. What happened after Kate's wedding?
   a. People were still interested in Kate.
   b. Kate decided to live in the spotlight more.

4. How does Kate use her fame?
   a. She brings attention to issues around the arts and health care.
   b. She brings attention to issues around security and the paparazzi.

5. Kate's engagement ring is also a reminder of a _____ event.
   a. happier
   b. sadder

C Watch the video again and match the words to create the phrases that are used in the video.

1. star   a. culture
2. pop   b. image
3. global   c. interest
4. fashion   d. power
5. commemorative e. icon
6. public   f. side
7. public   g. star
8. dark   h. products

D Answer these questions with a partner.

1. Do you find Kate Middleton's lifestyle appealing to you personally? Why or why not?

2. If you were in her position, what would you enjoy the most? What would you worry about? How would you use your fame?

3. If you ever met the Duchess of Cambridge, what questions would you ask her?

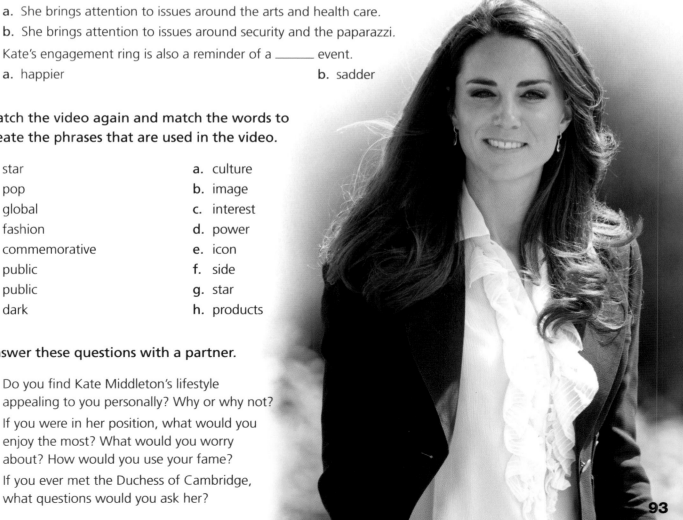

93

Writing

A Clearly stating your opinion is one way to strengthen your persuasive writing. You are going to practice this now by writing your opinions about an issue. Follow these steps first:

1. Read the question about celebrities and then read the two opposing opinions.
2. Which opinion do you agree with more and why? Discuss with a partner.

Do celebrities have a responsibility to act as good role models?

✓ YES

I think celebrities have a responsibility to act as good role models. The world is more "wired" than it was ten or twenty years ago. Before we had the Internet, it used to be easier for celebrities to lead private lives. Nowadays, however, with news about almost everything a simple click away, celebrities are watched more than ever. This means that if they make a mistake, the public sees it right away. Celebrities' bad behavior then has a terrible influence on the values of our society because people like to imitate celebrities.

✗ NO

I don't think celebrities have a responsibility to act as good role models. People become celebrities because they can sing or act or kick a ball well. They don't become famous because they have good behavior. Look at Lady Gaga, for example. She is known around the world because of her catchy pop songs. I think people go to her concerts to see her sing, not to watch her behave a certain way. In my opinion, what she does in her private time should be her own business.

B Read the Writing Strategy. Then look at the paragraphs in Exercise **A**. Which sentences are facts? Which ones are opinions? Discuss your ideas with a partner.

> **Writing Strategy**
>
> **Balancing Facts and Opinions** When you write an opinion piece, it is helpful to include both facts and opinions. **Facts** are true statements that can be proven.
> *The Duchess of Cambridge is married to Prince William.*
>
> **Opinions** are statements that the writer believes to be true. They may not be true for someone else.
> *She is the most stylish woman in the world.*
> State your opinions, and then use facts to support your opinions. By doing this, you make your argument stronger.

C Look at the opinions in the chart below. Which ones support the "yes" position in Exercise **A**? Which ones support the "no" position? Complete the chart with a fact that supports each opinion. (Refer to the examples provided for guidance.)

Opinion	Fact
1. Gossip TV shows and websites are highly effective at reaching impressionable, younger consumers.	1. *I know many teenagers who watch "Celebrity Talk," a very popular TV show that gossips about TV and movie stars.*
2. Many people enjoy reading about celebrities, but it's not likely people will imitate them if they behave badly.	2. *A famous athlete in my country got arrested several times for speeding. He plays for my favorite team, and I really like him, but I don't imitate his behavior.*
3. People see celebrities getting in trouble for bad behavior, but rarely suffering the consequences of their behavior. That sends a message that it's OK to behave badly.	3. _____
4. It is not a celebrity's responsibility to teach us how to behave; we each have to take responsibility for our own actions.	4. _____

D Using your notes in Exercise **C**, write two more paragraphs supporting either the "yes" or the "no" position in Exercise **A**. Use a separate piece of paper.

E Exchange papers with another student. Read your partner's writing and answer Questions 1–3 in the Writing Checklist.

Writing Checklist

1. Were the points clear?
2. Did the writing contain both facts and opinions?
3. Did the facts support the writer's opinion?

Expanding Your Fluency

What do you think of these kinds of die-hard fans? Discuss with a partner.

People who . . .

- wait in line for ten hours or more to see their favorite stars
- paint their homes or rooms in the colors of their favorite teams
- cover their rooms with posters of their favorite stars
- watch sporting events at all hours of the day and night
- get cosmetic surgery to look like their favorite stars
- pay a month's salary for an autograph of their favorite stars
- send letters and presents to their favorite stars
- name their children after famous athletes or celebrities

Ask

Answer Would you consider doing any of the things listed above? What is one outrageous thing you've done (or would like to do) as a fan?

Check What You Know

Rank how well you can perform these outcomes on a scale of 1–5 (5 being the best).

_____ use reported speech to report questions

_____ use key words to summarize a writer's ideas

_____ consider the advantages and disadvantages of fame

_____ write an opinion piece that is supported by facts

? Did you know?

Celebrity memorabilia has sold for unbelievable sums in recent years. Here are two examples:
most expensive piece of clothing: dress worn by actress Marilyn Monroe; sold for $1,267,500
most expensive lock of hair: from singer Elvis Presley; sold for $115,000

9 To Your Health!

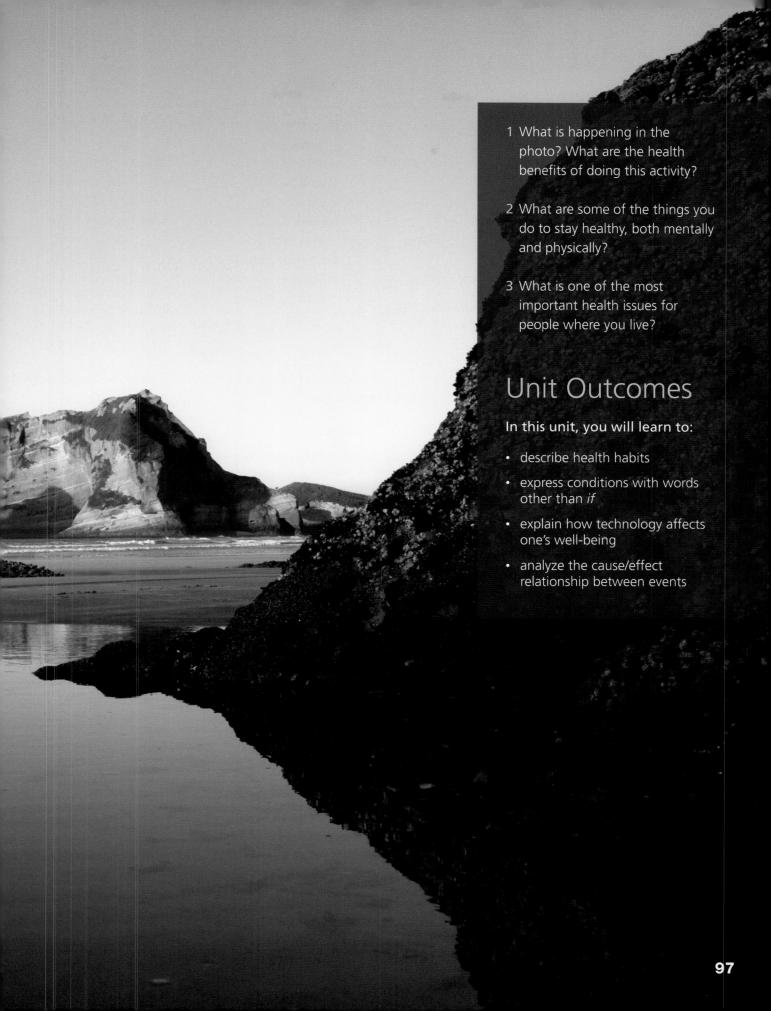

1 What is happening in the photo? What are the health benefits of doing this activity?

2 What are some of the things you do to stay healthy, both mentally and physically?

3 What is one of the most important health issues for people where you live?

Unit Outcomes

In this unit, you will learn to:

- describe health habits

- express conditions with words other than *if*

- explain how technology affects one's well-being

- analyze the cause/effect relationship between events

Vocabulary

addicted unable to stop doing something or using a chemical substance

automatic doing something without having to think about it

boost to increase

cranky irritable, in a bad mood

distracted not focused because you are thinking about other things

habit something that you do regularly or often without thinking about it

Expressions with *habit*: break/kick a ~, get into the ~

incentive something that encourages you to act a certain way

reinforce to support or make something stronger

revert to go back to an old habit or way of doing something

routine a habit; something you do regularly at the same time

substitute to replace one thing for another thing

willpower self-discipline; strong determination to do something

Expressions with *routine*: break the ~, get into a ~, get out of a ~, stick to a ~

A Read sentences 1–3. These people are trying to develop or break a habit. Which solution(s) can help each person's problem? Discuss your ideas with a partner.

Problems	Solutions
1. Jill: "I'm trying to get in shape, but I don't have the willpower to exercise alone."	a. Substitute something new (e.g., sugar-free gum) for the thing you've given up (e.g., cigarettes or soda) so you don't revert to the old behavior.
2. Sam: "I get easily distracted and have a hard time studying, which is creating a lot of stress for me."	b. Ask a friend to join you. It'll boost your motivation and help you reach your goal.
3. Yeny: "The reality is that I'm addicted to caffeine. I've tried to stop drinking coffee, but then I'm tired and cranky all the time."	c. Give yourself an incentive ("If I do *x*, then I can have *y*."). When you achieve that goal, reward yourself.
	d. Develop a routine and then stick to it for two weeks. This will reinforce the behavior so that it becomes automatic.

Sam needs to give himself an incentive to study. He should try working for an hour and then reward himself by taking a ten-minute break.

B What's a habit that you'd like to break or get into? Tell your partner. He or she will suggest a strategy that you could use and explain how this might be beneficial.

I'd like to find time to exercise for thirty minutes every day.

I'd like to quit smoking.

Caffeine, a highly addictive substance, is found in a number of foods and drinks.

Grammar

Stating Conditions: Other Ways of Expressing *If*

Conditions	Meaning
❶ I can take a break **(but) only after/only if** I study for an hour. I can take a break **provided that/as long as** I study for an hour.	I can take a break if (and only if) I study for an hour.
❷ I'll be sleepy **unless** I have a cup of coffee first.	I'll be sleepy if I don't have a cup of coffee first.
❸ You should set your alarm. **Otherwise**, you won't wake up on time in the morning.	If you don't (set your alarm), you won't wake up on time.
❹ I wouldn't join that gym, **even if** you gave me a free membership.	Nothing can make me join that gym, even a free membership.

❶ The words in bold express that one thing must happen first (studying) in order for another thing to happen (taking a break). Note that expressions with *only* can be preceded by *but*.
❷ *Unless* introduces a condition (having coffee) that will prevent a possible outcome (being sleepy).
❸ After a suggestion (set your alarm), *otherwise* shows what the result will be if the person does not follow the suggestion (you won't wake up on time).
❹ *Even if* is used when a result (I wouldn't join that gym) stays the same whether or not something else (you gave me a free membership) happens or is true.

A Choose the correct word or phrase to complete each opinion or situation.

1. a. It's hard to quit smoking **unless / only if** you take some medicine to help you.
   b. You can quit smoking on your own, **as long as / even if** you've got enough willpower.

2. a. **Even if / Only if** you're a vegetarian, it's still possible to get enough protein.
   b. **Only if / Unless** you eat meat, it's impossible to get enough protein in your diet.

3. a. **Only if / Unless** I get eight hours of sleep, I don't do well in class.
   b. I'd better get eight hours of sleep tonight, **otherwise / as long as** I won't do well in class.

4. a. I'm not distracted by texts from friends **provided that / unless** I turn off my phone.
   b. I need to turn off my phone. **Even if / Otherwise** I'm distracted by texts from friends.

B Now check your answers to Exercise **A** with a partner and answer these two questions.

1. Which sentence pairs (a and b) are similar in meaning? Which aren't? Explain.
2. Which statements do you agree with? Which do you disagree with? Why?

C Complete the sentences and then share your ideas with a partner.

1. I get distracted when I'm trying to study or work unless _____.
2. _____ if you have a lot of willpower, it can still be hard to _____.
3. Students in this class are allowed to _____ provided that _____.
4. It's important to _____. Otherwise _____.

Listening

> **disrupt** to prevent something from functioning in its normal way
> **REM (rapid eye movement)** deep, dreaming sleep
> **sleep deprivation** a serious lack of sleep

A You are going to listen to an interview about sleep. Read the Listening Strategy and then the outline below. With a partner, try to predict some of the answers.

> **? Did you know?**
> The longest a person has ever gone without sleep under supervised conditions is eleven days!

The Importance of Sleep

A Hours needed

- Adults (1) _____ hours
- Teenagers (2) _____ hours

B Risks of sleep deprivation

- (3) _____
- (4) _____
- (5) _____

> **Listening Strategy**
> **Using Visual Aids** Study any visual aids provided (e.g., an outline, charts, diagrams, maps) before you listen to see if you can predict what the speaker might say. This can help you follow and understand more of what you hear when you listen.

C Role of sleep in memory and learning

- Sleep (6) _____ things we've learned and transfers that information to (7) _____ memory.

D Things that disrupt our sleep

- Causes: (8) _____, (9) _____, (10) _____, (11) _____
- The main cause: (12) _____

B Listen to the interview and complete the outline.

C Read the questions below. Then listen again and answer the questions on a separate piece of paper. When you're done, check answers with a partner.

1. Who tends to get sleepy later at night? What's the result?
2. Explain what these statistics mean:
   a. four hours sleep/a 70% chance   b. one in five adults   c. 100,000 accidents
3. The speaker compares the brain and the sleep process to an e-mail in-box. How are they similar?
4. Where shouldn't you watch TV or movies in the evenings? Why?

D Discuss the questions with a partner.

1. Do you think you have healthy sleep habits? Explain using your answers from Exercises **B** and **C**.
2. In addition to the items listed in the outline, what other things can disrupt our sleep? How many of these have you experienced? Which is the hardest to deal with?

Connections

A Read the three scenarios. Then get together with a partner, and answer the questions below on a separate piece of paper.

Samir is studying English in the UK and is sharing a dorm room with another student. Samir tends to be a **morning person**; he usually **turns in** around 11:00 p.m. and gets up by 7:30 a.m. to make his first class. His roommate, on the other hand, is a **night owl**: He likes staying up late watching movies and talking on the phone. Samir doesn't mind this routine as long as his roommate is quiet by midnight. Unfortunately, he's been staying up until 2:00 or 3:00 a.m. recently, and Samir can't sleep. Unless things change, Samir feels like he's going to go crazy.

While in college, Emiko got into the habit of staying up late. She recently graduated and has gotten her first job; the problem is that she needs to be at work by 7:30 a.m. She's tried going to bed earlier, but she can't fall asleep. She **tosses and turns** for hours, and in the morning she **sleeps through** her alarm. She's been late for work three times this month, and once there she tends to be distracted and cranky for the first hour. Her boss told her that things need to change, otherwise she needs to find another job.

Pedro has a high-pressure sales job and works long hours. To help him stay energized, he started consuming several energy drinks every day. Though they initially gave him a boost, within an hour or two, he would **crash** and need to drink another. Worried about becoming addicted to the drinks and gaining weight from the sugar, Pedro decided to substitute with tea, but the drop in caffeine has left him feeling **drowsy**, especially in the afternoon. Unless he reverts to his old habit, Pedro doesn't know how he's going to be able to do his job.

1. What do you think the expressions in **bold** mean? Use your dictionary to help you.
2. What is each person's problem? What can each person do to solve his / her sleep problem?

B Choose one of the scenarios and create a short role-play in which you do the following:

Student A: Take the role of Samir, Emiko, or Pedro; in your own words, explain what your problem is.
Student B: Listen, ask questions, and offer your friend some advice.

C Perform your role-play for another pair. What do you think of the other pair's solution? Will it work? Why or why not?

D Switch roles and repeat Exercises **B** and **C**.

Reading

A Read the questions below and discuss them with your partner. Use your dictionary to help you understand the boldfaced words.

- If you were sick with a throat infection, would you be more likely to take **prescription** medicine or to drink a tea made of **herbs** to help cure it?
- Why might people prefer one **remedy** over the other?

B Read the article. Then mark each sentence below as *True* or *False*. Rewrite the false statements on a separate piece of paper. Check your answers with a partner.

1. Audra Shapiro almost died from eating a poisonous plant.
2. Up to half of all prescription drugs have been made from or inspired by plants.
3. The number of people using medicinal plants has declined in recent years.
4. Sometimes people take herbal medicines that make them sick. Scientists call this "the placebo effect."
5. Scientist Jim Duke opposes using plants to treat illness.
6. The people selling medicinal plants in Madagascar's marketplace know a lot about using them to treat illness.
7. Unless things change, many of Madagascar's medicinal plants may be lost.

C Match a word in bold in the article with a definition below.

1. curing _____
2. join _____
3. originated _____
4. man-made _____
5. got better _____
6. reducing _____

D Discuss these questions with a partner.

1. The article says, "the demand for nonprescription botanical drugs is on the rise." Why do you think this is?
2. You read about the placebo effect in the article. Do you think the mind and the "power of positive thinking" help people get better when they are sick? Explain.
3. A lot of health foods and products are advertised as "natural," "organic," or "doctor recommended." Discuss the meaning of these terms with your partner. Then give some examples of products for which these claims are true.

> Lemurs are one of the many species of flora and fauna that can only be found in Madagascar. How many natural remedies are hidden in this unique habitat?

Nature's Prescription

Leukemia survivor Audra Shapiro and her mother.

1 In Washington, DC, twenty children are attending a birthday party at a neighborhood park. The guest of honor, nine-year-old Audra Shapiro (pictured), is smiling as she opens presents and her mother takes photos. She and her parents have a lot to celebrate. Two years ago, Audra was diagnosed with leukemia;[1] today, though, she is cancer-free. She **recovered** from this disease thanks in part to a plant that originated halfway around the world.

Until very recently, Audra's disease would have
10 meant certain death. Now the long-term survival rate for childhood leukemia is above 90%, thanks to a drug made from a plant called rosy periwinkle, native to the African nation of Madagascar. In the last few decades, plants have contributed to the development of 25%–50% of all prescription drugs used in the United States alone. Some of these plant-**derived** medicines, like rosy periwinkle, are used to treat life-threatening illnesses like cancer. Others, like willow tree bark,[2] were originally used to make a very common pain reliever: aspirin.

20 Today, almost two-thirds of the people on our planet rely on the **healing** power of plants, and even in industrialized countries, the demand for nonprescription botanical[3] drugs is on the rise. In spite of this, there is still widespread debate about the effectiveness of using plants to treat illness. While many plants, like rosy periwinkle, have been the subject of extensive study and their effects are well documented, data on others are unclear. Scientists are often unable to determine which chemical or combination of chemicals within a plant is
30 responsible for **alleviating** pain, improving blood flow, or boosting one's mood. In addition, no one knows to what extent the placebo effect causes these changes: Sometimes people expect natural remedies to make them feel better, and, as a result, they do, whether or not the substance actually was responsible for this.

Despite the debate, it is generally agreed that plants contain important chemicals, many with beneficial effects. Jim Duke, a scientist who has spent years studying medicinal plants, is working to gather data to
40 help overcome the opposition to plant remedies. "We can **merge** science with herbalism," Duke says. "This will give us better drugs than if we only rely on ones we create ourselves. We can use science to test plants, to find what works best. The issue is not nature versus science; rather it is how to use science to get the best medicine, be it natural or **synthetic**."

[1] **leukemia** a cancer of the blood
[2] **bark** the material on the outside of the tree
[3] **botanical** related to plants

▶ **Rosy periwinkle**, the plant so important in Audra's leukemia treatments, is one of more than ten thousand known plant species—many of them with medicinal properties—in Madagascar. Originally, this was the only place in the world where you could find many of these species. Many of them are for sale every morning at the outdoor marketplace in Madagascar's capital. Here, vendors selling different medicinal plants function not only as salespeople, but also as doctors and pharmacists. Their knowledge comes from experience with plant remedies passed down from generation to generation. Many of the plants they use can be found all over the island, but this is changing. Now, forested land is being destroyed by population pressures, and a significant number of Madagascar's plant species are in danger of extinction.

Rosy periwinkle

Video

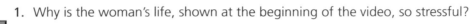

> **burnout** physical or emotional exhaustion caused by prolonged stress
> **chronic** constant; nonstop
> **neurons** brain cells
> **power through** (*informal expression*) to use all your energy and will to accomplish something, often quickly, despite difficulties
> **prone** having a tendency to be affected by something, usually in a negative way
> **resilience** the strength and ability to recover quickly from something bad

A Look at the two photos on this page. In both, the people are experiencing "stress." What's the difference? Discuss with a partner.

B Watch segment 1 of the video and then discuss the questions with a partner.

1. Why is the woman's life, shown at the beginning of the video, so stressful?
2. How does she say she handles it? Do you think this is a good idea? Why or why not?

C Read the outline below, and try to predict some of the answers with a partner. Then watch segment 2 and complete each blank with one word.

Stress hormones can . . .

- give us (1) _____,
- strengthen the ___immune system,___
- improve (2) _____, and
- help (3) _____.

Negative stress causes neurons to (4) _____ and change shape.

The results include . . .

- (5) _____ loss,
- greater (6) _____ and aggressiveness,
- signs of (7) _____,
- speeds up (8) _____, and
- more prone to (9) _____.

If we're unable to manage stress, the result can be (10) _____.

> **⚙ PRONUNCIATION** Notice how Teresa Pahl says, "I have a three o'clock call." at the beginning of the video. She pronounces *have a* as /hæv ə/. For more on reducing high-frequency function words to schwa, see p. 148.

D Watch segment 2 again and check your answers in Exercise **C**. When you're done, summarize the information in the outline. Then answer these questions with a partner: According to the report, how can we alleviate stress? When we do this, how does it affect our brains?

Ask

Answer Do you know anyone who's been under a lot of stress recently? Have they been affected in any of the ways mentioned in the video? Explain.
Can you think of other things a person can do to alleviate stress?

Speaking

A Read the text below. Then discuss the question with a partner. Use the prompts and explain your answer.

The news segment in the video talked about technology creating new sources of stress for some people. The reporter suggested that being connected to others 24/7 via phone, text, and e-mail can be unhealthy. What do you think?

- I don't think it's a problem at all.
- It's not a problem unless / as long as _____.
- It might be a problem, but only if _____.
- I think it's a problem. You can't _____, otherwise _____.

B Look at some examples of other ways that technology has the potential to impact our physical and mental well-being. Use one of the prompts from Exercise **A** to discuss your opinion of each situation with a partner. If you do think it's a problem, explain what you would do about it.

1. You see a man walking down a crowded street and texting at the same time. He's about to reach the end of the sidewalk.
2. You see a father with a baby carriage talking on the phone. He seems distracted by the call and does not seem to be paying attention to the baby.
3. Recently, two of your friends "unfriended" you on a social networking site.
4. Every time you go into your brother's or sister's room, he / she is playing video games. He / She often sleeps with a laptop next to the bed.
5. You're working on a paper for one of your classes and are researching some of the information on the Web. So far, your search has returned 250 relevant articles.
6. At your job, you have to sit for eight to nine hours a day in front of a computer.
7. your idea: _____

It's a problem only if he lets go of the carriage.

Even if he doesn't let go, his attention should still be on the baby.

C Discuss the questions with a partner.

1. Have any of the situations in Exercise **B** ever happened to you?
2. Do you think it's possible to become addicted to technology? Why or why not?

Writing
Describe Cause and Effect

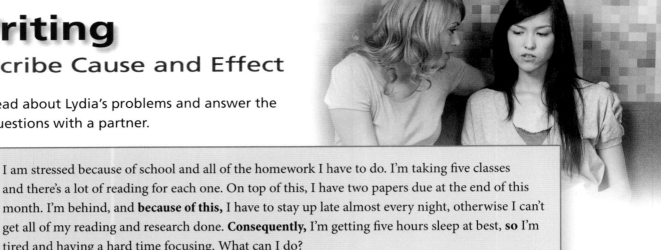

A Read about Lydia's problems and answer the questions with a partner.

> I am stressed because of school and all of the homework I have to do. I'm taking five classes and there's a lot of reading for each one. On top of this, I have two papers due at the end of this month. I'm behind, and **because of this,** I have to stay up late almost every night, otherwise I can't get all of my reading and research done. **Consequently,** I'm getting five hours sleep at best, **so** I'm tired and having a hard time focusing. What can I do?

1. Why is Lydia feeling stressed?
2. What kind of advice would you give to help her deal with this situation?

B Now read Vanessa's advice to Lydia. Do you think it is helpful? Discuss with a partner.

> I think that there are steps you can take to minimize the stress you're feeling. One thing I'd recommend doing is to create a work schedule for the rest of the month. For each day, list all of your "must-do" tasks first (eat meals, attend class, sleep, etc.). By listing the "must-do" tasks first, you'll get a sense of how much time you have available each day to devote to your homework, **therefore** you'll be able to plan your time better. Once you have listed all of your "must-do" tasks for each day, schedule the homework you have to do. **Since** you will probably need more time to research and write your two papers, try to schedule longer blocks of time (perhaps on weekends). Also, remember to schedule short breaks after you've worked for an hour or two. Knowing that you can take a break will give you an incentive to keep working. Creating this kind of schedule will help you stay focused and use your time more effectively. **As a result,** you will feel calmer and hopefully accomplish all you need to do this month. Good luck!

C Read the Writing Strategy and then answer this question: What's been challenging or stressful for you recently? (School, work, friends, something else?) Explain in a short (six- to eight-sentence) paragraph what specifically is stressful about your life at the moment, using cause/effect words and phrases.

Writing Strategy	**Showing Cause and Effect** When providing support for your opinions and ideas, explaining cause and effect can make your arguments stronger.

To show the **result** or **effect** of something, use: *as a result, consequently, therefore,* and *so.*
> I have a lot of homework. **As a result,** I stay up late.

To show that one thing **causes** another, use: *because/since, because of/on account of.*
> **Because/Since** I have a lot of homework, I have to stay up late.

D Exchange papers with a partner. Read your partner's paragraph and then write a paragraph of practical suggestions. Use the paragraph in Exercise **B** as a model. Be sure to state your suggestion(s) clearly and explain in detail what to do and why you think it will work using cause/effect words and phrases.

E Exchange papers again with your partner. Does your partner's paper state the suggestion clearly and describe in detail what to do? Does it use cause/effect words to explain why the solution will work?

Expanding Your Fluency

A Work with a partner. Are you familiar with the medical technology pictured? If you could invent a medical product or technology, what would it be and why? Together, choose an idea from the list below or come up with your own.

Our product will cure, correct, or control . . .

aging   memory problems   shyness   stress   other: _____

Put together a short presentation explaining your ideas. Make sure you also address these questions:

- How would this technology benefit people? What would the results be?
- How would it work? (i.e., Would it be a machine, a pill, a brain implant, something else?) How often would people have to use it (only once, several times, every day)?
- What would you call it?

B Present your idea to another pair. As you listen, take notes on the other pair's presentation and then answer these questions: Can you think of any possible drawbacks to the technology? Would you support its development? Why or why not?

Bionic limbs and other body parts will eventually enable the blind to see, the deaf to hear, and people to use damaged arms and legs again.

Check What You Know

Rank how well you can perform these outcomes on a scale of 1–5 (5 being the best).

_____ describe health habits

_____ express conditions with words other than *if*

_____ explain how technology affects one's well-being

_____ analyze the cause/effect relationship between events

107

10 Our Most Precious Resource

1 Read the unit title and look at the photo. Why is water our most precious resource? Do you think people take it for granted?

2 Make a list of the different ways people use water every day. Which are necessary? Which could we live without?

3 What is a story involving water that has been in the news recently?

Unit Outcomes

In this unit, you will learn to:

- refine your use of articles
- use key words to identify a speaker's purpose or attitude
- prepare and present a proposal
- write a formal e-mail message

Vocabulary

accumulate to collect something together over time

adequate enough

conserve to use something carefully so it lasts a long time

contaminate to make something dirty or harmful

dwindle to decrease in number

freshwater water that is not salty

have access to (something) to have something available to see or use

purify to make something clean

restore to return something to its original (usually better) state

scarce limited; in short supply

shortage a lack of something

toxic poisonous

A Work with a partner to complete the sentences with a number from the box. One number is used twice. Then check answers at the bottom of the page. Was any of the information surprising? Which statistic concerns you the most? Why?

| 1 | 2.5 | 50 | 70 | 5,000 |

? Did you know?

1. Though oceans cover almost _____% of the Earth, only about _____% of the water on our planet is potable (drinkable), and about two-thirds of that is water frozen in glaciers. The result: Less than _____% of the planet's water is available to meet our needs, and supplies are dwindling.

2. Almost _____ billion people today don't have access to clean drinking water. In parts of Africa, water is so scarce that people must walk several miles every day to get it.

3. Experts predict that almost _____% of the world will soon be facing water shortages of some kind. Our challenge, they say, is to restore our freshwater reserves and to conserve the water so that we have adequate supplies now and in the future.

4. Almost _____ people become ill every day from toxic substances that accumulate in rivers and streams and contaminate the water. Luckily, there are a number of ways to purify water so it's safe.

B On another piece of paper, add to the chart with words from the box. Work with a partner. Can you add other ideas?

| boil | conserve | evaporate | melt | mineral | pour | purify | spill | tap |

Types of water	Things we do to water	Things water does
bottled, drinking/potable, muddy	contaminate, run, sip, waste	freeze, soak (something)

C Discuss the questions with a partner.

1. Why do you think water is scarce? Why do some people have no access to clean water?

2. If we have water shortages in the future, where do you think we will get our water?

3. What can we do to protect water now and in the future?

Grammar

> **astonishing** very surprising
> **epic** very large and impressive

A Choose three sentences from the list below that are grammatically incorrect. Discuss why they are incorrect with a partner.

1a **People** need access to clean water.
1b **A person** needs access to clean water.
2 **The** Amazon River, **the** second longest in the world, starts in **the** Andes Mountains of Peru.
3a Water shortages are **a modern kind** of **problem**.
3b Water shortages are **a modern kind** of **a problem**.

4a Water shortages often hurt **poorest**.
4b Water shortages often hurt **the poorest**.
5a We learned about **water** in science class.
5b We learned about **the water** in **the science** class.
6a Colorado is **very dry** in **winter**.
6b Colorado is **a very dry** place in **the winter**.

Articles: *A/An*, *The*, and No Article (Ø)

a/an vs. the	Use *a/an* for count nouns in general or when we mention something for the first time.
	A: *Do you have **a** pen I can borrow?* (Any pen will do.) B: *Sure, here you go. When you're finished, just leave **the** pen on my desk.*
	Use *the* for specific nouns the speaker and listener already know about.
	*Can you turn off **the** faucet? **The** water is running.* (We both know these things.)
	*I think I left **the** car keys in **the** bathroom.*
the vs. Ø	Use Ø (no article) to talk about people or things in general. Use *the* to talk about particular people or things.
	In parts of Africa, water is scarce.
	*Most of **the** water we use is for cooking and bathing.*

B Complete this profile with *a/an, the*, or Ø. Then check answers with a partner.

Perth, (1) _____ capital of (2) _____ Western Australia, is at (3) _____ center of global climate change. This wasn't always the case, however. Decades ago, Perth was (4) _____ sleepy town with (5) _____ small population. But then everything changed, as (6) _____ resources in (7) _____ area (such as (8) _____ iron and (9) _____ gold) were mined and sold on (10) _____ world market. Then (11) _____ money came into the city, and (12) _____ population grew. With more people, the demand for water grew, especially in (13) _____ summer months.

That was fine . . . until recently. Due to climate change, the winds that usually brought (14) _____ heaviest rains to Perth moved south. Due to water shortages, (15) _____ city started to pump groundwater. Unfortunately, this is creating (16) _____ epic water crisis—people are pumping the groundwater faster than Mother Nature can replace (17) _____ supply.

C Complete these questions with *a/an, the*, or Ø. Then ask and answer them with a partner.

1. What is _____ water problem in Perth?
2. What should _____ city do to address this kind of _____ problem?

Listening

faucet a device that controls the flow of water from a sink or bath; the tap

mercury a metal used in thermometers

rust a brown substance that forms on metals that come in contact with water

A Listen to these four audio clips. What is the context for each one? Write your ideas.

1. some kind of _____ about water
2. a conversation between _____ and _____
3. a conversation between two people who are getting ready to _____
4. a lecture to people who work in the field of _____

> **Listening Strategy**
>
> **Listening for the Speaker's Purpose**
> Listen for key words that tell you about the speaker's <u>purpose</u> for speaking or the speaker's <u>attitude</u> (how he or she is feeling) while speaking

B Listen to the clips again. Write down key words you hear. Then choose the best answer to complete each sentence.

Recording 1 key words: _____

1. The purpose of the program is to educate viewers about **using water wisely at home / saving money on water / recycling water**.

Recording 2 key words: _____

2. The woman feels **angry / frustrated / relieved** about the water situation.

Recording 3 key words: _____

3. The woman thinks bottled water is **inexpensive / practical / wasteful**.

Recording 4 key words: _____

4. The purpose of this lecture is to tell the listeners which kinds of fish are **affordable / safe / tasty** to eat.

C Read the questions in column A. Then listen to the audio clips again and take notes using a separate piece of paper. When you're done, discuss the questions in column B with a partner.

Recording	A	B
1	What suggestion does the man make? How does it work?	Can you think of other ways to conserve water?
2	Why does the woman feel this way?	Could you fix the pipes in your house if you had to?
3	Why does the woman feel this way about bottled water?	Do you agree with her? Why or why not?
4	What issue is the speaker warning listeners about?	Have you heard about this issue before?

Connections

A Do you think water shortages are a serious problem? Why or why not? Are water shortages a problem where you live? Share your ideas with the class.

B Imagine you work for the Environmental Protection Agency in the country pictured. There are three urgent water issues that you must address. Do the following:

1. On your own, read about the three issues in the boxes below. Then . . .

   • rank the issues by priority (1 being the most urgent). Which should you address first, second, and third? Why?

   • think of at least one solution for each issue. What's the most effective way to deal with each issue?

2. Get together with a partner and discuss the questions above. Together decide what you will do.

 Drought Warnings: Rainfall in the middle part of the country has been low for the last three years. You're expecting that there will be widespread water shortages this summer, and you want to encourage people to start conserving now; otherwise you expect that people will lack adequate supplies during the summer months. The cost of informing the public through radio, TV, Internet, and advertisements could be almost 60% of your budget, though.

 Oil Spill: The southeastern coast of the country—the site of a large fishing industry—has recently suffered a big oil spill, which has contaminated the coastal waters. As a result, many in the region no longer have access to clean water. In fact, a number of people and animals have become sick from drinking local water. Citizens must be educated about purifying water to prevent widespread illness.

 Water Wars: A suburb in the north, just outside the capital, is home to several vacation resorts and a large golf course. The resorts provide many jobs and generate a lot of tax revenue. Meeting the water needs of this suburb has been challenging, though. The region gets very little rainfall, and most of the water for the resorts is brought in from smaller cities nearby. The result is that water in those smaller towns is becoming scarce. Citizens in the smaller towns are demanding changes.

C Get together with another pair and present your ideas. As you listen, take notes on a separate piece of paper. Then, discuss which ideas you think are the best and write them on the board.

D Review your classmates' ideas, and then together vote on the best course of action.

Reading

A Discuss the questions with a partner.

1. What are some of the best-known bodies of water (lakes, rivers, seas, etc.) or other water landmarks (beaches, dams, waterfalls, fountains, etc.) in your country? In the world?

2. Look at the photos in the article. Can you name these places? Do you know where they are? Scan the article quickly to find out.

B Read the article and then match the descriptions (1–10) with the correct place. Some descriptions match to both places. One description will not be used.

	Cara Blanca	Victoria Falls
1. shared by two countries	☐	☐
2. known for exceptional water color	☐	☐
3. used in the past for religious purposes	☐	☐
4. surrounded by forests	☐	☐
5. named for a famous queen	☐	☐
6. recently contaminated by toxic waste	☐	☐
7. in a region inhabited by humans for thousands of years	☐	☐
8. contains animal fossils	☐	☐
9. threatened by development	☐	☐
10. connected to a series of underwater caves	☐	☐

C Locate the words below in the article, and for each word write a simple definition or synonym. Try to work out the meaning on your own. Then check your answers with a partner.

1. *exposing*
2. *carry out*
3. *vast*
4. *plunges*
5. *dubbed*
6. *indigenous*

D You and a partner will create radio advertisements for each place mentioned in the article. First, decide who will do which place. Then work individually to create a thirty-second radio advertisement about why it is a good place for a "vacation getaway." Mention where it is, what makes it special, what you can do there, and other interesting facts. When you are finished, read your advertisement to your partner.

Ask

> **Answer** 1. Places like those in the article are vulnerable to pollution and overdevelopment because of tourism. What can be done to protect them while still allowing people to visit?
> 2. If you could visit only one of these places, which would it be? Why?

Majestic Waters

The Blue Pools of Belize

Located in the Cara Blanca region of Belize are twenty-three freshwater pools that are an intense blue color seen almost no other place on Earth. The pools in the Belize rainforest are a type of sinkhole[1] called a *cenote*, which forms when the roof of an underground cave collapses, **exposing** the water to the surface. These types of pools are found primarily in Mexico and Belize, with more than two thousand of them on the Yucatan Peninsula alone. For centuries, cenotes have been a main source of fresh water for people in the region.

Dr. Lisa Lucero, an expert on Mayan[2] civilization and history, has been studying cenotes for years. She has been doing research on the twenty-three pools in Belize and believes they were an important site to the ancient Maya, who believed cenotes were passageways to the underworld.[3] The pools may have been considered a holy site where people came to give birth or to **carry out** purification ceremonies, says Lucero. Recently, divers visiting pool 16—the bluest of all of the pools—discovered something else. The twenty-three cenotes form a **vast** underwater cave system whose walls are lined with crystals. Thirty feet below the surface of the water, divers also discovered fossils of huge animals, which they believe are mammoths or saber-tooth cats that lived 25,000 to 30,000 years ago along with humans. Others think the Cara Blanca fossils may be even older than that—they could be dinosaurs from millions of years ago.

Victoria Falls: A Natural Wonder

Victoria Falls, located in the African nations of Zimbabwe and Zambia, is a UNESCO World Heritage Site and one of the Seven Natural Wonders of the World, and it's easy to see why. The waterfall is one of the largest and most inspiring in the world. Water from the Zambezi River **plunges** almost 354 feet (108 meters) over a ledge of lava[4] rock. The falls generate mists[5] that can be seen from more than 12 miles (20 kilometers) away. Famed Scottish explorer David Livingstone **dubbed** this waterfall Victoria Falls (in honor of the British queen of the same name). Its **indigenous** name, Mosi-oa Tunya, means "the smoke that thunders." Surrounding the falls are forests thick with mahogany, fig, palm, and other plant species. Fossils found near the falls show that early humans may have lived here two million years ago. More modern tools have also been found—evidence of far more recent settlements (fifty thousand years ago).

Today thousands of visitors from around the world visit Victoria Falls each year, and the area is at risk of tourism-based development as more resorts, restaurants, and hotels open. Operators in the area offer everything from helicopter flights over the falls to bungee jumping, and providing these activities while preserving the environment is an ongoing challenge.

[1] **sinkhole** a hollow place or depression that collects water
[2] **the Maya** a civilization based in southern Mexico and northern Central America that prospered from 600 BCE to 900 CE
[3] **underworld** the place where spirits of the dead live
[4] **lava** hot liquid rock that comes out of a volcano
[5] **mist** large number of tiny water droplets in the air, which creates a kind of fog

? Did you know?

Though Victoria Falls is one of the largest waterfalls in the world, it is not the tallest. Angel Falls in Venezuela at 3,212 feet (979 meters) is the tallest.

Video

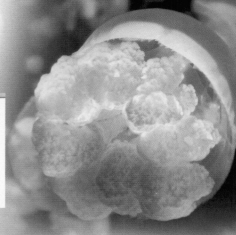

algae plants with no stems or leaves that grow in water
glide to move in a quiet and smooth way
propel to push or move something forward
seep to flow slowly and in small amounts (liquids and gases)
symbiosis relationship between two different organisms that benefits both

A You're going to watch a video about the golden jellyfish of Jellyfish Lake.
Read the words in the word bank and the quick facts. Then discuss the questions with a partner.

1. What do you think the connection is between the jellyfish and the algae?
2. Why do you think the jellies spend each day following the sun from one side of the lake to the other?

The golden jellyfish has a large bell on top of its body which it uses to propel itself forward in the water.

Quick Facts about the Golden Jellyfish
• Millions of jellyfish, also called "jellies," live in Jellyfish Lake.
• Each day the jellyfish follow the movement of the sun, migrating from one side of the lake to the other.
• Many jellyfish have a dangerous sting to protect themselves. The jellyfish in Jellyfish Lake have evolved in isolation (developed separately from other animals), so they've lost their sting.

B Watch the video and then answer the question.

What main question does the video answer?

a. Why are the jellyfish endangered?
b. Why do the jellyfish follow the sun?
c. How do jellyfish protect themselves from predators?
d. Why are the jellyfish golden in color?

C Read the questions. Then watch the video again and answer the questions.

1. How did the jellyfish arrive in the lake? _____
2. Complete the summary. Then answer Questions 1 and 2 in Exercise **A**.

Tiny algae _____ the jellies' bodies. The algae turn _____
into _____. This _____ the jellies. As a result, the jellyfish care
for the _____. At dawn, the jellyfish move _____, toward
the _____.

D In terms of natural beauty, do you think that Jellyfish Lake is similar to the places in the reading on page 115? Discuss your answers with a partner.

Speaking

A Read about Crystal Pools, once a popular vacation spot. In the past, what kind of place was it? Whom did it cater to? What happened to it? Why? Share your ideas with the class.

Crystal Pools

- Located along a coastal area known for its clear blue waters, Crystal Pools was for years a popular destination for local and international vacationers. It featured several pools, high-end dining, and luxury accommodations.

- Over time, the economy slowed, and the number of people who could afford Crystal Pools dropped significantly. The resort was also criticized for being out of character with the natural environment and for contributing to the destruction of wildlife in the area. In time, the owners sold the property, and recently Crystal Pools closed.

B Work with a partner. You are investors who want to buy and restore Crystal Pools. You plan to open it to the public again. What makes you think that your new establishment will be successful? What makes it different from other resorts? Use the questions below to help you put together a presentation about your new establishment.

1. What will be the concept of your new establishment? Will you use the original concept or design something new? Why? What will you call your place?

2. What sort of customers do you aim to attract (families, businesspeople, budget travelers, partygoers, luxury vacationers, ecotourists, something else)?

3. What sort of accommodations will you offer (a large hotel, small villas or cottages, outdoor tents, underwater suites, something else)?

4. Which of the following will your new establishment offer?

   - golf course
   - live entertainment
   - meeting facilities
   - restaurants
   - spa and fitness center
   - swimming pools
   - outdoor activities
   - cooking classes
   - other: _____

C Present your business plan to another pair. Take notes on what they tell you. At the end, tell them what you liked about their plan; also suggest ways that they might improve it.

> **TIP** You can use visuals (a handout or slideshow with key text, photos, and other graphics) to structure and support your presentation. You can elaborate on this information when you speak to your audience.

D Repeat Exercise **C** with another pair. At the end, review your notes. Which establishment (yours or another pair's) has the best chance of success? Why? Share your answer with the class.

Writing
E-mail for Formal Communication

A Read the e-mail that a Korean woman named Young Ju sent to an Italian woman named Chiara. Then discuss the questions with a partner.

1. Why is Young Ju writing to Chiara?
2. Is Young Ju's message formal or informal? How do you know?

Hi Chiara,

Your friend Lisa Harris and I are classmates at Columbia University. She told me that you live in Venice, and she suggested that I contact you. I'm going to be visiting your city for five days later this month, and here's why I'm writing: **Can you** recommend a few sights to see while I'm there? (**FYI: I** don't speak Italian!) I'm going to be staying at a hotel near the Piazza San Marco, so **can you** suggest one or two things to do in that area? Actually, Lisa mentioned that just walking around is great (as long as there are no floods!). She said it's so **cool** to explore the canals, find a cafe, and **chill out** for an hour or two. I'm really excited to see a city built entirely on water! Is a gondola ride worth **checking out? And one last thing:** Could you also suggest a couple of good restaurants in the city? I like all kinds of food.

Thanks a lot for your help! **Hope to hear from you** soon.

Young Ju

B Match the boldfaced expressions in the e-mail with their formal equivalents in the chart. Then, read the Writing Strategy and rewrite Young Ju's message so that it is more formal. Compare e-mails with a partner.

More formal	More informal
Dear Chiara,	Hi,/Hey,/the person's name only (*Chiara,*)
I'm wondering if you could . . . / I'd appreciate it if you could . . .	
Just so you're aware . . .	
Nice	
Relax	
Seeing	
Finally	
Thank you so much.	
I look forward to hearing from you.	
All the best,/Best,	Take care./Your name only (*Young Ju*)

Writing Strategy

Using Appropriate Register

In more formal e-mail messages: (1) certain openings (*Dear Chiara; Dear Ms./Mr. Walker*) and closings (*All the best; Warm regards*) are typically used; (2) longer sentences are typically used, especially if one is making a request (*I'm wondering if you could . . . ; I look forward to hearing from you soon*); (3) abbreviations and texting conventions (like *BTW, FYI*) are not used. In very formal situations, contractions, such as *I'm*, are spelled out. (4) colloquial words and expressions or slang (like *chill out, check out, one last thing*) are not used.

118 Unit 10

C Read the information and then write an e-mail to Dr. Luca Damore on a separate piece of paper.

> Venice is beautiful, but its residents are tormented by frequent floods that can make life in the city difficult. You are an urban planning major who wants to do an internship this summer. Your professor, Christina Strand, gave you the name of her colleague, Dr. Luca Damore, and suggested contacting him. Dr. Damore is currently leading an initiative to help the city plan for flooding and minimize its effects. He needs a volunteer research assistant this summer. You think this would be a great opportunity since you're interested in the contact points between cities and the environment, and Venice is such a unique case. You'd like more information about the position. You also want to know if fluency in both English and Italian is required for the internship.

In an e-mail to Dr. Luca Damore . . .

1. introduce yourself and explain how you found out about the internship.
2. request the information noted.
3. remember to use a formal tone throughout your message.

D Exchange papers with a partner, and read your partner's e-mail. Is it clear what the writer is asking for? Is the tone formal enough? What can the writer do to improve?

Expanding Your Fluency

Read the six situations (a–f) below. Then do steps 1 and 2 with a partner.

1. Come up with a simple definition for each underlined word or phrase.
2. Use at least one of the words or phrases and other vocabulary you learned in this unit to write a short dialog on a separate piece of paper. Then perform your dialog for another pair.

a. The teacher found out that Bill cheated on the exam, and now Bill is really <u>in hot water</u>.
b. You'll never know what it's like to live on your own unless you just <u>take the plunge</u> and do it.
c. Ten thousand dollars might seem like a lot of money, but for a wealthy man like Mr. Jones, it's <u>a drop in the bucket</u>.
d. That restaurant is known for its <u>mouthwatering</u> dishes and relaxing atmosphere.
e. It's been a stressful day. I think I'm going to go for a run and <u>let off some steam</u> before I go home.
f. For a long time Carlos and his brother didn't get along, but that's all <u>water under the bridge</u>. Now they're the best of friends.

Check What You Know

Rank how well you can perform these outcomes on a scale of 1–5 (5 being the best).

_____ refine your use of articles

_____ use key words to identify a speaker's purpose or attitude

_____ prepare and present a proposal

_____ write a formal e-mail message

11 Inspired Minds

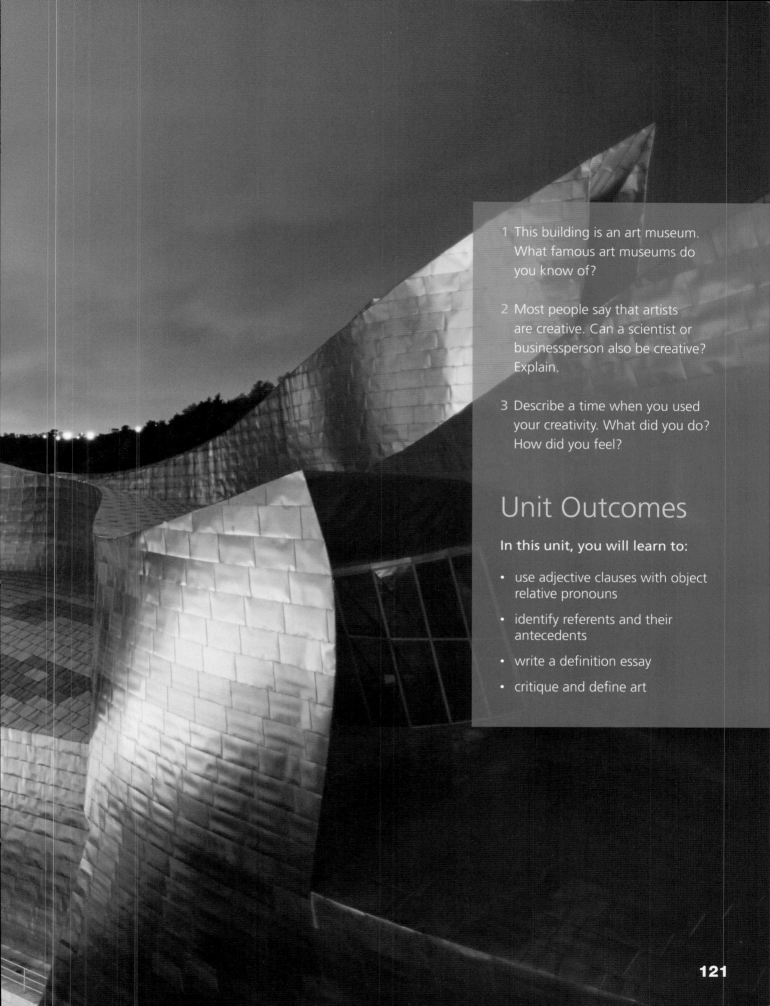

1 This building is an art museum. What famous art museums do you know of?

2 Most people say that artists are creative. Can a scientist or businessperson also be creative? Explain.

3 Describe a time when you used your creativity. What did you do? How did you feel?

Unit Outcomes

In this unit, you will learn to:

- use adjective clauses with object relative pronouns
- identify referents and their antecedents
- write a definition essay
- critique and define art

Vocabulary

breakthrough an important development or achievement

faulty not made correctly or not working properly

fixated thinking about something to an extreme and excessive degree

frustrated feeling upset or angry because you are unable to do anything about a problem

impasse a difficult situation in which further progress is not possible

in a flash (happening) suddenly and for a very short time

insight a clear, deep, and sometimes quick understanding of something complex

stage part of an activity, process, or period

wander to stray in movement or in thought

Word Partnership

How many expressions can you find that use the words *mind* or *idea*? Underline them in Exercise **B**. What do they mean?

A Read the insight puzzle below. Work with a partner and try to solve it. Stop after three minutes. Were you able to solve the puzzle?

A man and his son are in a serious car accident. The father is killed, and the son is rushed to the hospital. The doctor looks at the child and says, "I can't operate. This child is my son!" How can this be?

B Read about Marta's experience with the puzzle. Choose the correct option for each item. Did you have a similar experience? Discuss with a partner.

After reading the puzzle, I quickly ran through a lot of ideas that didn't work. Soon I reached a(n) (1) **impasse / breakthrough** and felt "stuck." I had run out of ideas. I then chose one of the ideas and tried to make it work. I (2) **frustrated / fixated** on the idea and returned to it again and again, even though it clearly wasn't working. I couldn't come up with any new ideas and felt (3) **insight / frustrated**. At this (4) **stage / breakthrough**, I paused for a few moments and took a break. My mind was (5) **wandering / faulty** a bit and even though I still had the puzzle in the back of my mind, I found myself easily distracted. It felt as if my mind was clearing itself of (6) **frustrated / faulty** ideas. In a flash, everything changed. I experienced an "aha moment." I had a sudden (7) **breakthrough / impasse** and the answer to the puzzle came to mind.

C Discuss these questions with a partner.

1. What did you think of the insight puzzle in Exercise **A**? Have you ever experienced a big "aha moment"?
2. Think of a time when you were frustrated because you were at an impasse. What did you do?
3. By letting her mind wander for a bit, Marta was eventually able to think better and find a solution to a problem. Do you ever do this?
4. Creative thinkers often say that their breakthroughs come to them in a flash. Practical thinkers say they fixate on one idea and don't give up until they've made it work. Which kind of thinker are you? Give an example.

Grammar

A Mark all the sentences that are correct.

a. I'll never forget the puzzle that I couldn't solve.

b. I'll never forget the puzzle which I couldn't solve.

c. I'll never forget the puzzle I couldn't solve.

d. One puzzle, that I couldn't solve, made me frustrated.

e. One puzzle, which I couldn't solve, made me frustrated.

f. One puzzle, I couldn't solve, made me frustrated.

Adjective Clauses with Object Relative Pronouns

	Describing People	Describing Things
❶ Restrictive clauses	The most creative person **who(m)/that/Ø** I know is my mother.	The computer **which/that/Ø** I use was obviously designed by a creative thinker.
❷ Nonrestrictive clauses	My best friend, **who(m)** I've known since childhood, is very creative.	This computer, **which** I bought last week, was obviously designed by a creative thinker.

❶ These clauses give <u>necessary information</u> about the object. They complete the meaning of the sentence. In restrictive clauses you can also omit the relative pronoun: *The most creative person I know is my mother*. The relative pronoun *that* is only used with restrictive clauses.

❷ These clauses give <u>extra information</u> about the object. You don't need them to complete the meaning of the sentence. They are separated from the main clause by commas. You cannot omit the relative pronoun.

B Complete the sentences with the correct relative pronoun. Some sentences may have more than one correct answer or no pronoun at all (Ø). Then, discuss with a partner. Were you surprised at the results of the creativity study? Why do you think it turned out that way?

1. The university _____ I attend was doing a two-part study on creativity.

2. A professor _____ I knew from my psychology class asked me to join it.

3. For the first part of the study, five friends, _____ I'd brought with me, were split into two groups.

4. We then tried to solve some insight puzzles _____ the researchers gave to us. One group was placed in a red room, the other in a blue room.

5. The group _____ the researchers placed in a red room didn't do so well.

6. The other group, _____ was placed in a blue room, solved twice as many puzzles as the red group.

7. For the second part of the study, a comedy performance, _____ I hadn't seen before, was shown to three of us. The other three didn't see it.

8. My group, _____ the researchers asked to go first, did better than the other group.

9. The researchers, _____ I respect a lot, were not surprised at the results.

C On a separate piece of paper, combine the two sentences into one by making an adjective clause. Do you agree with these statements? Discuss with a partner.

1. Creativity is a special talent. You are born with it.

2. "Being practical is more important than being creative" is a statement. I agree with it.

3. Most of the people in this class are creative. I enjoy coming to this class.

Listening

accent (color) a secondary color used to emphasize
intense very great or extreme in strength or degree
tranquility a peaceful, calm state

A Look at this floor plan of a home. Imagine you have to paint these rooms. Discuss with a partner.

B Now listen to an interview with Annie Cho, decorator and color expert. What color does she recommend for each room in Exercise **A**?

1. bedroom
2. home office
3. kitchen
4. dining room
5. living room

a. blue
b. green
c. lavender
d. red
e. yellow

C Listen again. Complete these tips from Annie.

General advice

1. Because painting your home can be _____, start with _____ room.
2. Ask yourself: What kind of _____ do I want to create?
3. Don't get _____ on one particular color and _____ it.

Specific advice

4. People are more _____ in blue rooms.
5. Orange is a _____ color, but it can be kind of _____.
6. Yellow is a nice choice because it gives you _____.
7. Red encourages people to _____ more; that's why many _____ use it.
8. Don't use red in a room where you have to _____.
9. Lavender _____ your nerves and encourages _____.

Ask
Answer

Based on Annie's advice, what colors do you think Gary is going to paint his rooms? Why? Use your notes from Exercises **B** and **C** to explain. Would you follow Annie's advice? Why or why not?

Connections

> **design** to plan and draw an object so that it can be built or made
> **logo** special visual design or writing of a company's name that is used on products and advertising
> **slogan** short phrase that is easy to remember

A Read about a famous logo and its designer. Then answer the questions with a partner.

1. Who designed the logo, and who was it for?
2. How did the designer get the idea?
3. Why do you think the design is one of the most imitated designs in the world?

In the1970s, graphic designer Milton Glaser was given a job. He was asked to design a logo that the city of New York could use in an advertising campaign to attract tourists to the city. He went through several stages and in the end, he settled on a safe and clean design: the words "I love New York" on a white background. He submitted the design, which everyone seemed to like, but he wasn't satisfied with it.

 Days later, while riding in a taxi and not thinking about anything in particular, he pulled out a piece of paper and started drawing. In a flash, he had a breakthrough. He saw the design clearly in his mind: I ♥ NY. This logo is still one of the most recognized and imitated designs today.

B Work with a partner. You are going to design a logo and slogan for a city's advertising campaign. If your logo does not include a slogan in it, as the example in Exercise **A** does, be sure to add one. Use a separate piece of paper.

1. Choose a city that you both know.
2. Design the logo by doing the following:

 • Choose a primary (main) color and an accent color, as well as any other colors you want to use. (Remember what you learned about the use of colors.) Draw a logo.
 • Think of a slogan: It should be a catchy phrase, short and memorable.
 • Use letters and/or symbols in your slogan.

C Get together with two other pairs and explain your logo and slogan. Use the sentences below to comment on the other pairs' designs.

1. Their design uses a logo that people will identify with _____ [name of city] immediately.
2. The colors that they chose for this design are _____ because _____.
3. People will find the slogan, which is _____ and _____, to be _____.
4. I think people who see this design will want to visit _____ [name of city] because _____.

D Take a vote. Which design is your favorite?

Reading

The *Mona Lisa*

masterpiece an extremely good painting, novel, movie, or other work of art

mural a large picture painted on a wall

priceless worth so much money that the value cannot be estimated

A Do you recognize this painting? What do you know about Leonardo da Vinci? Discuss with a partner.

B Look at the title, image, and subtitle of the article. What do you think it is about? Discuss with a partner.

C Read the article. Then read this list of events and put them in chronological order.

_____ a. Maurizio Seracini finds the clue "*Cerca trova*" in Vasari's mural.

_____ b. Seracini finds evidence that there is another painting behind Vasari's mural.

_____ c. Leonardo da Vinci paints the mural *The Battle of Anghiari*.

_____ d. Seracini's team finds a hollow space behind Vasari's mural.

_____ e. The project is put on hold again, even though evidence suggests that the painting under Vasari's mural might be a da Vinci.

_____ f. Giorgio Vasari is commissioned to renovate the Hall of 500 and paints the mural *The Battle of Marciano*.

_____ g. Seracini's team is given permission to investigate the mural for one week.

> **Reading Strategy** | **Identifying and Understanding Referents**
>
> Writers use pronouns and other words to refer back to a previously mentioned word, phrase, or idea. They do this to avoid having to repeat the same words again and again.

D Read these excerpts from the article. Match the underlined referents (1–6) to one of the answers (a–d).

a. da Vinci's works (in general)   b. the hidden mural   c. the *Mona Lisa*   d. Vasari's mural

_____ 1. (lines 16-17) . . . may wait in line at the Louvre art museum in Paris for hours to see <u>it</u>.

_____ 2. (lines 18-20) . . . combined with his historical and cultural importance, make <u>each and every one</u> of his works priceless.

_____ 3. (lines 40-42) Did Vasari build a false wall in front of Leonardo's original mural to protect <u>it</u>?

_____ 4. (lines 49-51) Additionally, even if there is another painting behind <u>it</u>, it is not certain that it would be a da Vinci.

_____ 5. (lines 55-57) . . . and the possibility that some of the paint used in <u>it</u> is the same paint used in the *Mona Lisa*.

_____ 6. (line 64-65) "If it's discovered, <u>it</u> would be one of the most famous discoveries of a century."

Ask

Answer A common expression in English is "the end justifies the means," which means even if the process isn't ideal, the result makes it worthwhile. What do you think about Seracini's project? Will the end justify the means? Why or why not? Discuss with a partner.

Lost Leonardo

The Palazzo Vecchio is one of Florence's most beautiful public spaces, but its most important masterpiece isn't even there anymore . . . or is it?

1 Maurizio Seracini is a man on a mission. He is an expert in Italian art from the University of California, San Diego, and he has been working on a project in the Palazzo Vecchio in Florence for over thirty years. When he stands in the Hall of 500, he doesn't see the breathtaking, sixteenth-century mural by Giorgio Vasari; he sees the possible resting place of a lost work by Renaissance master Leonardo da Vinci.

Leonardo da Vinci was born in Italy in 1452.
10 While he is known as a painter, geologist, inventor, scientist, and architect, da Vinci can perhaps be most accurately described as a creative genius.[1] Although he made significant advances in many fields of study, he is most remembered for his contributions to the world of art. Today, visitors hoping to see his most famous masterpiece, the *Mona Lisa*, may wait in line at the Louvre art museum in Paris for hours to see it. The diversity and quality of da Vinci's talents, combined with his historical and cultural importance, make each and
20 every one of his works priceless.

Ironically, in his own time, da Vinci's work was not always so well appreciated. In the 1550s, artist Giorgio Vasari was commissioned[2] to remodel the Hall of 500 and paint over Leonardo's existing unfinished mural, *The Battle of Anghiari*. However, according to one rumor, Vasari himself was a fan of da Vinci and didn't want to destroy the original work. Now,
30 almost five hundred years later, Seracini is finding clues that perhaps Vasari did not destroy Leonardo's masterpiece after all.

Seracini found his first clue in the 1970s, while examining a section of Vasari's mural, *The Battle of Marciano*. He found a strange inscription[3] on the work, *Cerca trova* ("Look
40 and you will find."). Did Vasari build a false wall in front of Leonardo's original mural to protect it? A radar scan did in fact detect a hollow[4] space behind the mural, strengthening the possibility that a lost da Vinci is hidden in plain sight.

Further investigation, however, has become difficult. The possibility that another painting might be just out of view is not sufficient evidence to authorize a search that might considerably damage Vasari's work, which is itself a masterpiece. Additionally, even if there is
50 another painting behind it, it is not certain that it would be a da Vinci. In 2011, however, Seracini was granted limited permission to drill into existing cracks in Vasari's mural. With only one week to complete the work, what they found was encouraging: definite evidence of a painting behind Vasari's original work and the possibility that some of the paint used in it is the same paint used in the *Mona Lisa*.

Seracini's project is currently on hold as he waits for permission to investigate further. The risk of
60 damaging Vasari's work is still a major concern that might prevent the project from moving forward. Still, the possibility of finding a lost da Vinci is worth the risk to many in the art world. According to art historian Martin Kemp, "If it's discovered, it would be one of the most famous discoveries of a century."

[1] **genius** a highly talented, creative, or intelligent person
[2] **commissioned** to be formally arranged to work for someone
[3] **inscription** something written by hand in/on a book, photograph, or painting
[4] **hollow** having space inside it (as opposed to being solid all the way through)

The Hall of 500 inside the Palazzo Vecchio

Video

> **graffiti** words or pictures that are drawn in public places
> **vandalism** deliberate damaging of things, especially public property

A Look at the images on this page. What do you see, art or vandalism? Why? Discuss with a partner.

B Choose the best synonym for the words in bold.

a. criticized	c. signature
b. dirty	d. surface for painting

_____ 1. A train tunnel in the nation's capital is a **gritty** gallery.

_____ 2. Nick Posada's work is here; "Tale" is his **tag**.

_____ 3. Even on such a public **canvas**, there are rules to be followed in the world of graffiti.

_____ 4. [Graffiti artists] are used to being **vilified**, and now they are being enjoyed.

C Watch the video on urban art and mark each statement *True* or *False*. Then, with a partner, correct the false statements on a separate piece of paper.

1. The Wall of Fame is a train tunnel famous for graffiti art.

2. Nick Posada thinks there is a difference between graffiti art and vandalism.

3. Nick is surprised that one of his pieces is still on the Wall of Fame.

4. The only place graffiti artists like Nick can show their work is in the streets.

5. Chris Murray sees a lot of similarities between graffiti art and traditional public art, since both are commissioned.

6. Graffiti art has sold well to collectors.

D The narrator mentions that even in public spaces, there are rules to follow in the world of graffiti. What do you think the rules are? Discuss with a partner. Then get together with another pair and share your rules.

Speaking

A What is art? Read this list of statements. Which ones do you agree with? Can you add to the list? Discuss with a partner.

True art _____.

- makes you think deeply
- should be seen in museums
- is beautiful

- takes a long time to create
- is made for an audience

- costs a lot of money
- is memorable
- can't be made by just anyone

- your idea(s): _____

PRONUNCIATION Changing the stress of a word(s) within a sentence can change the sentence's meaning. To stress a certain word you generally say it more slowly, clearly, and loudly. This gives emphasis to that word. Listen to the examples below.

True *art costs a lot of money.*
(as opposed to art that is ordinary)

*True art costs a **lot** of money.*
(emphasizes amount of money)

For more on the prominence of stress, see p. 149.

B Look at these pictures (including the graffiti). Which ones are art? Which aren't? Why do you think so? Discuss with a partner.

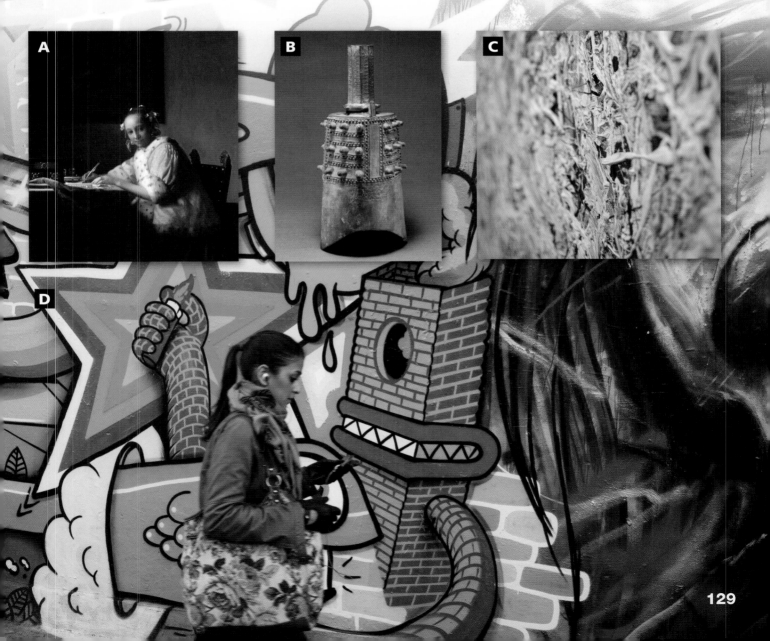

A

B

C

D

Writing
Write a Definition Essay

A   Read the essay. Then discuss the questions with a partner.

What is art? According to the *Collins Cobuild Dictionary,* "art consists of paintings, sculpture, and other pictures or objects that are created for people to look at and admire or think deeply about," but I don't agree with this definition completely. First of all, I don't think that art is always "created for people to look at." Recently, I was in a museum where I saw a vase that was over five thousand years old. The vase was used to gather water from the river. When the people made it, they weren't thinking about "art." But today we can appreciate the vase as part of a display in an art museum. Second, I think this definition is incomplete because it doesn't mention anything about skill. Art isn't something that just anyone can do in a short period of time. There is one part of this definition that I do agree with though. I think that art should make you think deeply. When you look at art, something should catch your eye and make you stop and wonder.

     Leonardo da Vinci was a talented artist who studied for many years to learn his skill. His *Mona Lisa* is a true work of art. In this painting, we see a woman posing for a portrait. It looks like an ordinary painting, but then something makes you stop and wonder. There is something about her facial expression; she seems to be smiling slightly. What could she be smiling about? It isn't clear and it makes you think.

1. Which part of the definition of *art* does the writer agree with? Disagree with?
2. What does the writer think about Leonardo da Vinci and his art?

The Louvre, the museum in Paris where the *Mona Lisa* is displayed

B   You are going to write about the word *creativity*. Look up the definition in a dictionary. Then read the Writing Strategy and outline your ideas in preparation for writing. Use the two-paragraph structure to write a definition essay.

> **Writing Strategy**
>
> **Writing a Definition Essay**   A definition essay explains the meaning of a term. Abstract terms, such as *love* or *art*, often work well because their meaning depends more on the writer's perspective than it does with more concrete terms, such as *book* or *chair*.
>
> **First paragraph**
> ❶ Introduce the dictionary definition at the beginning of your essay using one of these expressions:
>
>   *The dictionary defines* creativity *as . . ./According to the* (name of dictionary) creativity *is . . ./When you look up* creativity *in the dictionary it says . . .*
>
> ❷ Write about the parts of the definition you agree or disagree with. Give examples to support your views.
>
> **Second paragraph**
> ❸ Write about a specific piece of art you know. Describe the art briefly.
> ❹ Do you think it took a lot of creativity to create this art? Use your definition of the word *creativity* to support your opinion.

C   Exchange papers with a partner and read his or her essay. Do the paragraphs follow the points outlined in the Writing Strategy? What do you think of your partner's argument in the second paragraph? Do you agree with it? Why or why not?

Expanding Your Fluency

A Art doesn't have to be something found in a museum or gallery. In pairs, discuss the six groups below. Do you think any creations from these groups can be considered art? Which ones?

architecture (exterior and interior of buildings or rooms)

cooking (tasty or colorful foods)

fashion (interesting clothing, hair, or makeup)

landscape (picturesque places: gardens, public parks, etc.)

technology (gadgets of any kind)

transportation (fascinating bicycles and cars)

B Work in pairs and pick two groups from Exercise **A**. For each group, think of one example that could be considered a work of art. Make some notes on your examples so you can share with another pair. Use a separate piece of paper.

C Now get together with another pair. Take turns describing your two works of art to them, and then listen to their descriptions. Do you agree that their examples are art? Why or why not?

Ask

Answer What are some of the ways that you express yourself creatively?

Architecture can definitely be a work of art! Casa Milà, which was designed by Antoni Gaudi, is the perfect example because . . .

Check What You Know

Rank how well you can perform these outcomes on a scale of 1–5 (5 being the best).

_____ use adjective clauses with object relative pronouns

_____ identify referents and their antecedents

_____ write a definition essay

_____ critique and define art

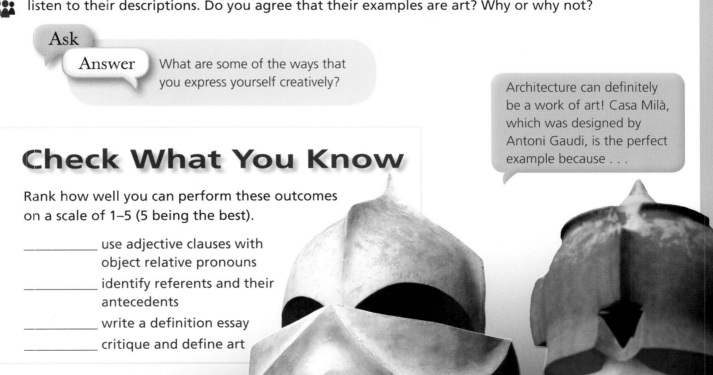

12 What's So Funny?

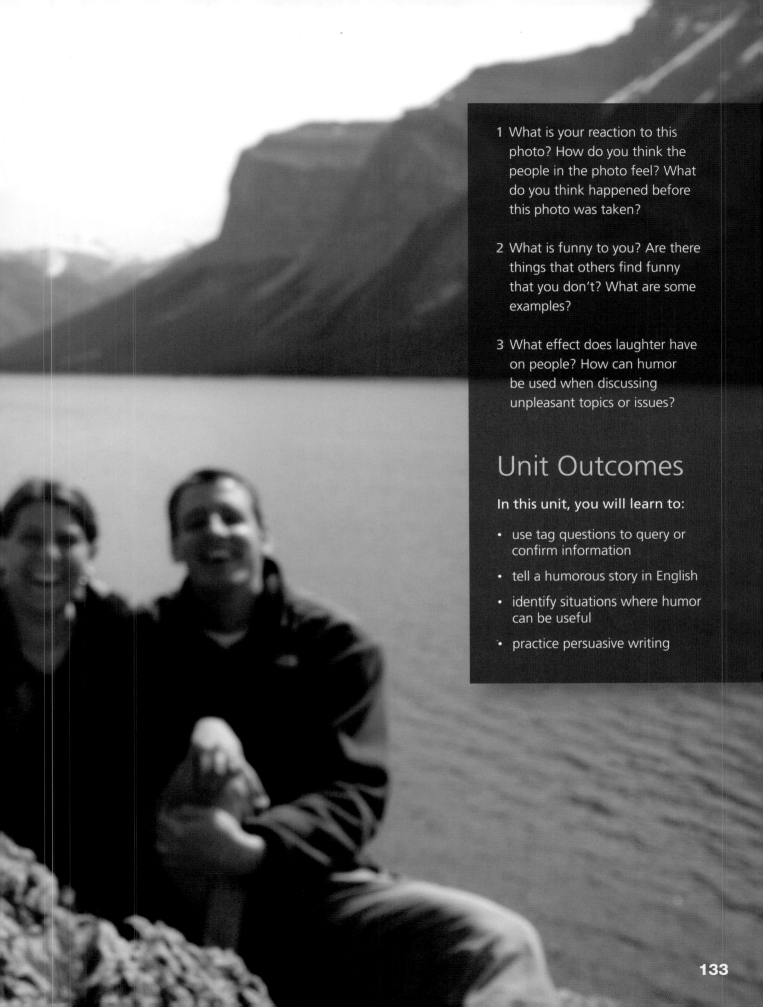

1 What is your reaction to this photo? How do you think the people in the photo feel? What do you think happened before this photo was taken?

2 What is funny to you? Are there things that others find funny that you don't? What are some examples?

3 What effect does laughter have on people? How can humor be used when discussing unpleasant topics or issues?

Unit Outcomes

In this unit, you will learn to:

- use tag questions to query or confirm information

- tell a humorous story in English

- identify situations where humor can be useful

- practice persuasive writing

133

Vocabulary

comedian an entertainer who tells jokes to make people laugh

delivery the way a joke or humorous story is told

exaggerate to indicate that something is bigger, worse, or more important than it really is

expose to uncover, reveal

hysterical extremely funny

kid to say something as a joke

off-color rude or offensive

offensive something that upsets or embarrasses because it is rude or insulting

point out to direct attention to something

profanity offensive language; swearing

punch line the words at the end of a joke that make it funny

shortcut a way that is more direct or quicker

universal related to everyone in a group, society, or the world

witty amusing in a clever way

> What other words come before or after *hysterical*?
> *just ~; absolutely ~; ~ laughter*

A Read this profile of comedian Jerry Seinfeld and choose the correct option for each item.

The Comedy of Jerry Seinfeld

Jerry Seinfeld, a stand-up comedian, is considered one of the best observational (1) **shortcuts / comedians** in America. An observational comedian makes (2) **witty / offensive** comments about what he or she notices in everyday life. This type of humor seeks to (3) **expose / exaggerate** the absurdity that most of us usually don't see until it is pointed out. Observational comedy is more about generating an "Aha!" moment from the audience, rather than telling straight jokes with punch lines.

Seinfeld is well known for his delivery—the way he uses the pitch of his voice to (4) **exaggerate / expose** and emphasize his points with a note of sarcasm. He is also admired by many for his "clean" material. Seinfeld has said of using off-color language: "Profanity is a great shortcut of comedy and the reason I don't use it is that I am concerned about the joke-quality suffering." He believes comedians can be funny without being (5) **hysterical / offensive**.

B In pairs, answer these questions.

1. What type of comedy does Seinfeld specialize in?
2. How does Seinfeld use his voice in his delivery?
3. What does Seinfeld think about the role of profanity in comedy? Do you agree?
4. What do you think of Seinfeld's approach to comedy? Can ordinary events be funny?

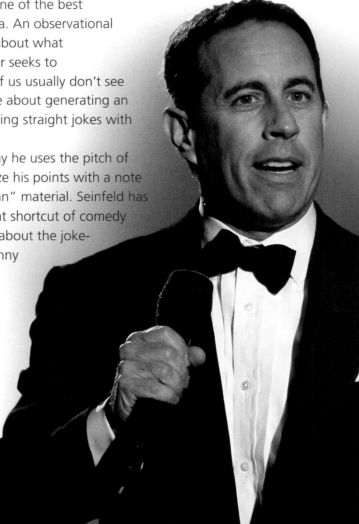

Jerry Seinfeld performing stand-up comedy in front of a live audience.

Grammar

Tag Questions

A tag question is a question added to the end of a statement. Tag questions are used to either confirm or query a conclusion. They often indicate the speaker's attitude about a topic.

Tag questions include a pronoun and an auxiliary verb. They comment on a preceding statement.	**You haven't** read that, **have you**? **We laughed** so hard at that joke, **didn't we**? **You think** so, **do you**?
Affirmative statement + negative tag = the speaker assumes that the listener agrees. The anticipated answer is "yes."	**He's** really funny, **isn't he**? (Anticipated answer: *Yes, he is funny.*) **You'll** come to the show tonight, **won't you**? (Anticipated answer: *Yes, I will come tonight.*)
Negative statement + positive tag = the speaker assumes that the listener agrees with a negative point of view. The anticipated answer is "no."	**She isn't** a very good actress, **is she**? (Anticipated answer: *No, she isn't.*) **They couldn't** understand the joke, **could they**? (Anticipated answer: *No, they couldn't.*)

In other contexts, tag questions can be used to anticipate disagreement or an emotional response. See p. 165 of the Grammar Summary for more details.

> You'll sometimes hear the ungrammatical expression *aren't I* in a tag question. This is common in casual speech.
>
> *I'm right, aren't I?*

A Complete the conversation with appropriate tag questions.

Liz: Hey, check out this shirt. It's really cool, (1) _____?

Jen: It's OK, I guess. The color reminds me of one Deidre has. You've seen her wearing it before, (2) _____?

Liz: The brown one? Yeah, I have. But Deidre's shirt looks nothing like this one. Hers has long sleeves, (3) _____?

Jen: I'm talking about the color. You wouldn't want to walk around looking like Deidre, (4) _____?

Liz: Actually, I don't really mind. She looked so pretty at the party, (5) _____?

Jen: You're right. There's nothing wrong with looking like Deidre, (6) _____?

B Role-play the situation from Exercise **A** with a partner. Add any extra details you think are necessary. Perform your role-play for the class.

PRONUNCIATION Most *wh-* questions use falling intonation, while *yes/no* questions use rising intonation. Which kind of intonation do tag questions use? For more on intonation in tag questions, see p. 150.

C Listen to the model conversation made up entirely of questions. Now have a conversation with your partner made up entirely of questions. You cannot repeat the same question, and you cannot ask one-word questions (such as *Why?* or *What?*). How long can you keep your conversation going?

Listening

in good/bad taste fitting (or not fitting) generally accepted social standards

stereotype to unfairly characterize all members of a certain group (ethnicity, nationality, gender, age, etc.) as being the same

A Do you laugh easily at jokes or does it take something really funny to make you laugh? What jokes do you find offensive or inappropriate? Why? Discuss with a partner.

B Listen to a conversation between a brother and sister on their walk home from a comedy club. Choose the correct answer.

1. Which speaker liked the show?
   a. Jocelyn   **b.** Nick   **c.** both

2. What reason does one speaker give for disliking the comedian?
   a. poor delivery   **b.** bad jokes   **c.** both

3. What would you say to describe a very funny joke?
   a. It's not in good taste.   **b.** It's hilarious.   **c.** both

4. Which parts of the comedian's material does one speaker dislike?
   a. profanity and punch lines   **b.** punch lines and stereotypes   **c.** profanity and stereotypes

5. Why doesn't Nick want to go to a comedy club with Jocelyn again?
   a. Comedy clubs are dangerous.   **b.** He might feel uncomfortable.   **c.** He has a bad sense of humor.

C Listen again. Then discuss these questions with a partner.

1. What arguments does Jocelyn make about the comedian's use of profanity? Do you think her views are justified?

2. What upsets Nick about jokes that use stereotypes? Are stereotypes always negative?

3. When Nick says, "Unfortunately we can't all have your amazing sense of humor," he is being sarcastic. What does he really mean?

4. Which speaker's opinions do you agree with most? Why?

Connections

A You are producing a new TV show. In the show, people are tricked into behaving foolishly in front of a hidden camera. Your writers have suggested the following situations. In pairs, read each situation and decide if the idea is genuinely funny or in bad taste. Mark whether you approve each suggestion and record your reasons for each decision.

Situation	Decision	Reasons
1. A piece of jewelry is slipped into a celebrity's handbag at an expensive boutique. A guard stops her, searches her bag, and finds the jewelry.	✓	This practical joke would be hilarious because celebrities are used to special treatment. She'll be very surprised, and her reaction will be funny for the audience.
2. A young woman is pulled over by the police and told that the car she is driving was reported as stolen.		
3. A child is given a new kitten. Later, the kitten is taken away.		
4. A teenage boy is told he has gotten the lowest score possible on the college entrance exam.		
5. The front wheel on a man's bicycle is loosened so it falls off while he is riding.		
6. A woman receives a call informing her that her husband has been in a bad car accident.		
7. A man tries to start his car, but the horn blows and all the lights flash. The car won't start.		
8. A couple is eating in a nice restaurant. The man begins to cough and suddenly seems to stop breathing.		

B Form a group with two other students and act as TV producers. Together, discuss each situation in Exercise **A** and agree on the three best ideas for the TV show. Was it difficult to reach an agreement? Why or why not?

> It's mean to take the kitten away, isn't it?

137

Speaking

A Get into a group of three students and follow these steps.

1. Think about something funny that happened to you or someone else. It can be a personal experience or come from another source, such as a movie, book, or the news. What happened exactly? What made it funny? Take some notes. Use the Story Outline to guide you.

2. Plan your delivery: Think about the tone of your voice, which words you will emphasize, and at which points you will pause in the story.

3. Take turns telling your story to your group.

4. When a speaker is done, ask him or her any questions you have. Then think about the questions below and take some notes.

Notes Checklist

- Did the speaker use 1) effective pauses and 2) word stress?

- What was the punch line? Which words were stressed?

- Was the story funny? Why or why not?

Story Outline
Subject: _____
Introduction: _____
Climax: _____
Conclusion: _____

B Discuss each story with the group. What made each one funny? Which story was the funniest? Why?

One time my dog did the funniest thing...

Video

A You are going to watch the Little Tramp in the film *The Immigrant*.
What kind of trouble do you think he will get into? What will he do
to make you laugh? Discuss with a partner.

B Watch segment 1 and mark each statement *True* or *False*.

	True	False
1. The woman and her mother are crying because they are sick.	☐	☐
2. The Little Tramp can't get the woman's attention.	☐	☐
3. The Little Tramp takes all of his money back from the woman.	☐	☐

C Watch segment 2 and choose the correct answer to each item.

1. Why does the captain stop the Little Tramp?

   a. He wants to steal his money.
   b. He thinks the Little Tramp is a thief.
   c. He wants to ask him the time.

2. How does the woman react when she finds the money?

   a. with horror
   b. with laughter
   c. with joy

3. Why does the woman cry at the end?

   a. She is thankful.
   b. She loses her money again.
   c. She dislikes the captain.

> Born in London in 1889, Charlie Chaplin was one of the first great movie stars. His work in silent films during the 1910's and onward made him a global icon. In the movie *The Immigrant*, Charlie Chaplin plays the Little Tramp, a poor man who moves to another country in search of a better life. Moviegoers laughed and cheered on the Little Tramp because they identified with his humble, everyman persona and loved to watch him overcome challenges.

D Watch segment 3 and put these events in order.

_____ a. The waiter knocks the Little Tramp's hat off.

_____ b. The Little Tramp blows his nose.

_____ c. The Little Tramp burns his mouth on his food.

_____ d. The Little Tramp's neighbor leaves the table.

_____ e. The Little Tramp finds a coin.

_____ f. The Little Tramp orders his food.

E Work with a partner and choose two or three themes from the list. Then explain how each issue is treated humorously in the video. Write on a separate piece of paper.

generosity	manners	social status
immigration	poverty/hunger	war

Ask

Answer In difficult moments, some people use humor to lighten the mood. Can you think of someone you know who is able to do this? How do they make you feel?

Reading

A Read the quotation below. What does this person mean?

Do you agree with him? Discuss with a partner.

"You can turn painful situations around through laughter. If you can find humor in anything, even poverty, you can survive it." —*Bill Cosby*

B Read the article. Then answer the questions below with a partner.

1. How can humor be used to make people feel better after a loss?
2. How does humor help people feel more comfortable with each other?
3. What is the relationship between humor and stress?

C Match each situation with one of the paragraphs (A–D) from the reading based on the topic. Not all paragraphs are used.

_____ 1. You have been studying for an important examination. Passing will help you get your dream job. You haven't slept well in recent weeks and are often irritable. Your friend hasn't seen you in a long time, so he/she stops by your place to cheer you up.

_____ 2. You are on a crowded elevator when it suddenly stops between floors and won't move. Someone calls for help, but in the meantime you are all waiting. The passenger standing next to you makes eye contact briefly. He mentions a movie where the same thing happens.

_____ 3. You are in the hospital recovering from a serious car accident. You have had several surgeries and will be missing at least one month of work. You are in a lot of pain and are unable to do things without the help of a nurse or your family. A relative comes to visit you and tells you a funny story about the last time she was in the hospital.

_____ 4. Your home and neighborhood have been completely destroyed in a flood. You have lost most of your belongings, but your family is safe. You are temporarily staying in a government shelter. A former neighbor sees you in the shelter and comes over to talk. He jokes that he has been meaning to renovate his house for years and it looks like now he'll have a real reason to.

D With a partner, choose one of the situations from Exercise **C**. Take one of the roles and act out the situation together. Think carefully about how humor could be used in the situation.

Ask

Answer You can use humor to make fun of yourself instead of others. This is called *self-deprecating humor*. How could this type of humor help make someone feel better?

Comic Relief
The Role of Humor in Society

A
1 Humor is a universal human trait. Everywhere around the world, people find things to laugh about, and sharing humor is an essential part of being human. Even in the darkest tragic drama, a writer might insert a scene that makes the audience smile or even laugh to break the tension. This is known as "comic relief." In real life, comic relief makes the world an easier and better place to live.

Humor as a Coping Mechanism[1]

B
There are taboos about making fun of some topics, such 10 as religion, death, and misfortune. However, humor is a tool people frequently use to lessen pain, sadness, and loss. People tell funny stories about a departed loved one at a funeral to remember the good things about them. They make jokes about being ill or poor to stop worrying. Humor is a way for whole societies, nations, or even the world to deal with a shared loss. Laughter lightens the weight of sadness.

▼ This man is dressed as a jester—a type of clown historically employed by royal families in Europe.

Humor as a Social Lubricant

C
Another role of humor is as a tool to ease social 20 awkwardness.[2] People tell a joke to begin a speech. They share funny stories with new acquaintances. Sometimes these stories are slightly embarrassing and they let listeners know that the person has let his or her guard down.[3] Most people enjoy the company of those who make them laugh. Laughter is also contagious.[4] One person's laughter can start a whole crowd laughing along.

Humor as Good Medicine

D
In recent years, scientific studies have begun to prove what many of us already knew—humor is good for you! 30 Studies have shown that humor and laughter are great ways to reduce stress; and reducing stress improves one's health. For example, the results of a recent report showed that finding humor in one's life leads to better mental and physical well-being. This was particularly relevant in the fight against heart disease. For years, medical professionals have used comedy and humor to improve their patients' ability to fight autoimmune disorders and to increase the speed with which they heal from injuries. It's a common saying that "Laughter is the best medicine," 40 and studies are increasingly showing that to be true!

[1] **coping mechanism** an action or effort intended to relieve stress
[2] **social awkwardness** feeling of embarrassment or difficulty in situations
[3] **to let one's guard down** to relax
[4] **contagious** likely to spread quickly in a group of people

Writing
A Persuasive Essay

A Read the information about the Ridiculam Prize and explain to a partner what it is.

> The Ridiculam Prize is presented each year to a humorist or comedian who has made outstanding contributions to understanding society through humor. Past recipients come from a wide range of backgrounds, including writers, actors, stand-up comedians, and cartoonists. With wit and courage, these people present a unique perspective on the issues of today. Not only do they make us laugh, but they challenge us to think a little deeper about what we are laughing about. Honorees go on a national tour to bring further attention to the issues they deal with in their humor.

B You are on the selection committee for the Ridiculam Prize. Who would you nominate? Think about the funny people you know personally or have seen on television. Why do they make you laugh? What social issues do they comment on? Make three selections and then discuss with a partner to narrow your choice to one final selection. (You and your partner do not have to chose the same person.)

C Read the sample essay below. Then write your own persuasive essay of at least three paragraphs explaining why your nominee should win the Ridiculam Prize. Use a separate piece of paper.

> If anyone deserves to win the Ridiculam Prize, it is humorist Stephanie Gavin. She is a successful writer and one of the funniest people I know. She is my nominee for this prize.
>
> For ten years, Gavin has written a humor column that appears in several national newspapers. She writes mainly about the funny little differences between men and women in society today. Her sarcasm allows readers to see these differences in a way they probably didn't before, and the fact that the people she jokes about still like her humor only proves how funny she is. For example, her article "Mr. Man" was just as popular among men as it was among women. She has written over fifteen books of humor and essays, of which six have become bestsellers. She has won numerous writing awards, and her material has been made into a popular TV show, *The Uptowners*. I have many of her books and reread them often. She never fails to make me laugh.
>
> I cannot think of another living humorist who has made so many people laugh. She is such a funny person and is extremely deserving of the Ridiculam Prize.

TIP Use specific facts, such as numbers or statistics or real examples, to make your argument stronger.

D Exchange your essay with another student. Was your partner's argument convincing? What can they do to improve it?

Expanding Your Fluency

A Read about different types of humor. Then, in pairs, try to come up with other examples of these types of humor that you have seen.

- A **parody** is a piece of work that makes fun of an original work (painting, book, movie, song, etc.).
- A **practical joke,** also called a **prank,** is a trick played on someone, often with the goal of slightly embarrassing them.

B Answer these questions. Then share your answers with a partner and explain your reasons.

1. Have you ever played a practical joke on someone?
   a. Yes, and it was hysterical.   b. Yes, and I regretted it.   c. No, I would never do that.

2. If someone played a prank on you, what would you do?
   a. I would laugh!   b. I would be irritated.   c. I would be furious.

3. Have you ever created or participated in a parody?
   a. Yes, and it was fun.   b. Yes, and I regretted it.   c. No, and I never would.

4. What do you think of parodies?
   a. They are really funny, and they can be good for the original work by keeping it relevant and popular.
   b. Sometimes they are funny, but sometimes they are disrespectful.
   c. They are disrespectful to artists and their works.

C Share your answers with another pair and then discuss. Why do you think so many forms of humor involve laughing at other people and their work? Do you think it's important to be able to laugh at yourself? Why or why not?

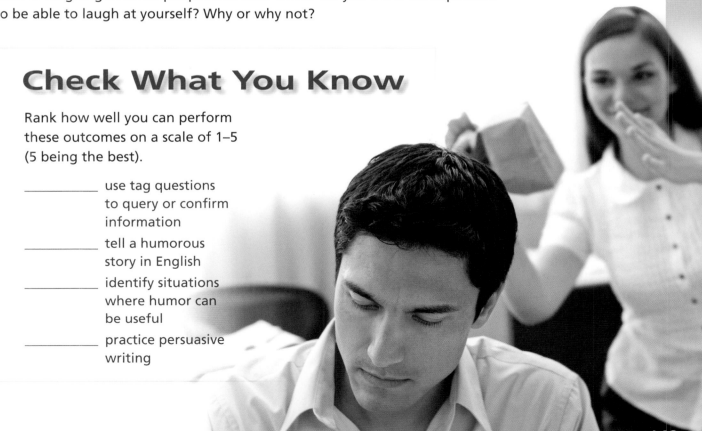

Check What You Know

Rank how well you can perform these outcomes on a scale of 1–5 (5 being the best).

_____ use tag questions to query or confirm information

_____ tell a humorous story in English

_____ identify situations where humor can be useful

_____ practice persuasive writing

Pronunciation

Stress on Content Words versus Function Words

 Most sentences contain content words and function words.

>The **effects** of **so** many **languages disappearing** could be a **cultural disaster**.

Content words carry meaning and are usually stressed, that is, spoken more clearly and loudly. Content words usually include key nouns and pronouns, main verbs, adjectives, and adverbs.

Function words usually do not carry meaning and are usually unstressed, that is, spoken more quickly and can be harder to hear in everyday conversation. Function words include articles, auxiliary verbs, conjunctions, determiners, prepositions, and pronouns.

Listen to the sentence and notice the difference in stress on content and function words.

>**Alice** was **beginning** to get **very tired** of **waiting** for the **bus** in the **rain**.

TIP Remember that words are not stressed simply because they are content words. Content words are stressed if they carry important meaning. Also, function words are sometimes stressed to draw the listener's attention to that particular word.

Practice

A Listen to the sentences. Mark the words that are stressed. How are they different than the unstressed words?

1. The baby slept well and is very happy today.

2. Cecilia enjoys surfing and rock climbing.

3. The doctor said that I have the flu.

B Identify the content words and function words in each sentence. Say the sentences with stress on the content words. Then listen and repeat to check your work.

1. The dogs are both wet from the rain.

2. Who went with you to the movies last night?

3. Natalie said that Ms. Norton is her favorite teacher.

4. I need to write a few more sentences to finish my essay.

5. That was the most beautiful sunset I've ever seen.

6. You must have run quickly to get here on time.

7. I've never eaten at that restaurant before.

8. Where did you learn to speak Portuguese?

9. My sister just gave birth to twin boys.

10. I'll have soup and salad.

Differences between American English and British English

Playwright George Bernard Shaw said that America and Great Britain are "two countries separated by a common language." The Americans and the British both speak English, of course, but there are some differences in grammar, word choice, spelling, and especially pronunciation. Below are some examples of the pronunciation differences.

Pronunciation			
Differences	**Examples**	**American**	**British**
letter *a*	ask, grass	/æsk/, /græs/	/ask/, /gras/
letter *r*	forty, board	/fɔrti/, /bɔrd/	/fɔti/, /bɔd/
intrusive /r/	idea of, saw a	/aidiə əv/, /sɔ ə/	/aidiər əv/, /sɔr ə/
-ery, -ary	cemetery, ordinary	/sɛmətɛri/, /ɔrdənɛri/	/sɛmətri/, /ɔrdɪnəri/

The intrusive *r* sound occurs in British English between a word ending in vowel sounds such as /ə/ and /ɔ/ and another word beginning with a vowel sound. In British English there is also a tendency to omit or reduce the vowel sound in the word endings *-ery* and *-ary*, producing /ri/ or /əri/ instead of /ɛri/.

There are also some differences in spelling patterns between British and American English. Note that these differences do not affect pronunciation.

Spelling

-or (Am) vs. -our (Br)	**-ize (Am) vs. -ise (Br)**	**-er (Am) vs. -re (Br)**
color/colour	recognize/recognise	center/centre
flavor/flavour	organization/organisation	meter/metre

Practice

A Listen to the two pronunciations of the words below. For each one, choose *Am* if the pronunciation is American English or *Br* if the pronunciation is British English. Check your answers. Then listen again and repeat.

1. **a.** staff   Am / Br   **b.** staff   Am / Br
2. **a.** short   Am / Br   **b.** short   Am / Br
3. **a.** military   Am / Br   **b.** military   Am / Br
4. **a.** agenda is   Am / Br   **b.** agenda is   Am / Br
5. **a.** banana   Am / Br   **b.** banana   Am / Br
6. **a.** record   Am / Br   **b.** record   Am / Br
7. **a.** extraordinary   Am / Br   **b.** extraordinary   Am / Br
8. **a.** stationery   Am / Br   **b.** stationery   Am / Br
9. **a.** thawing   Am / Br   **b.** thawing   Am / Br
10. **a.** secretary   Am / Br   **b.** secretary   Am / Br

Reducing to Schwa: *to*

Reduction occurs in spoken language when sounds are shortened and/or changed slightly. In English, the vowel sound in the word *to* is often reduced from /oʊ/ to schwa /ə/. For example:

- Elias covered his head with a towel <u>to keep</u> cool.
- My class ends at a quarter <u>to two</u>.

Often, this reduction occurs when *to* appears before the words *him* or *her*.

- I need to speak <u>to him</u> in the morning.
- The letter was addressed <u>to her</u>, not you.

This reduction also occurs when *to* is paired with other words, for example *ought*, *have*, and *going*.

- There <u>ought to</u> be a law against that.
- I would go to the party, but I <u>have to</u> do homework.
- She told me that she's <u>going to</u> start college in the fall.

Notice that in some of these cases, the /t/ sound in *to* disappears and the sounds in the other words also change.

> **TIP** Do not reduce the vowel sound in *to* to schwa when it comes before another schwa, for example:
> - He's going to give his furniture <u>to a</u> friend.

Practice

A Say each sentence aloud and then listen to the recording. Say the sentences again and then mark reductions of *to* in the sentences.

1. I was going to call Jim, but I forgot.
2. Why did you give my MP3 player to her?
3. Let's move to another table.
4. Ava has to get good grades to go on the trip.
5. That book is overdue, and I really need to return it.
6. We ought to report the accident right now.
7. Do you think we can get them to agree on a meeting place?
8. Gavin sent a birthday present to a friend today.
9. You don't have to drive very far to your office.

Intonation to Show Sarcasm and Irony

 Sarcasm is the use of **irony**, the opposite of what is actually meant, to be humorous or maybe even insulting. In spoken English, sarcasm is largely expressed by the way the words in a statement or question are said.

Listen to the sentences below. You will hear them read twice. The first time the intonation shows sincerity; the second time it shows sarcasm. Listen for the differences.

- He did a **great** job fixing your bike, **didn't he**?

- He did a **great** job fixing your bike, **didn't he**?

- That party was **so** much fun; I **can't wait** for the next one!

- That party was **so** much fun; I **can't wait** for the next one!

 TIP Remember that these are general tendencies that speakers follow when being sarcastic. There are no set pronunciation rules.

For more on tag questions see pages 135 and 150.

In the first example, notice how an overemphasis on the words *great* and *didn't he* stand out in the sarcastic sentence; the speaker does not think he did a great job fixing the bike. Likewise, the words *so* and *can't wait* are overemphasized in the second; the speaker did not have fun at the party and is not looking forward to the next one. That strong, expected emphasis on key words indicates that the speaker actually means the opposite of the literal meaning of what they are saying.

Practice

A Listen to the pairs of sentences. Choose *sincere* or *sarcastic* for each sentence based on the intonation.

1. This sure is great weather we're having!	**sincere / sarcastic**
2. This sure is great weather we're having!	**sincere / sarcastic**
3. Yeah, this is exactly like you said it'd be.	**sincere / sarcastic**
4. Yeah, this is exactly like you said it'd be.	**sincere / sarcastic**
5. Do you think you could say that a little louder this time?	**sincere / sarcastic**
6. Do you think you could say that a little louder this time?	**sincere / sarcastic**
7. Take as much time as you like.	**sincere / sarcastic**
8. Take as much time as you like.	**sincere / sarcastic**
9. This line is moving really quickly.	**sincere / sarcastic**
10. This line is moving really quickly.	**sincere / sarcastic**
11. It's such a surprise to see you here.	**sincere / sarcastic**
12. It's such a surprise to see you here.	**sincere / sarcastic**
13. She's already so popular, isn't she?	**sincere / sarcastic**
14. She's already so popular, isn't she?	**sincere / sarcastic**

B Practice saying the sentences with your partner. Focus on using intonation to be either sincere or sarcastic. See if your partner can guess which one.

Reducing to Schwa: High-Frequency Function Words

 As you already know, **reduction** occurs in spoken language when sounds are shortened and sometimes changed. **Function words** carry very little meaning, but have a grammatical role in the sentence. The vowel sounds in function words are frequently reduced to schwa in English.

Moira <u>can</u> help you with that.

The only model we have left is orange <u>and</u> green.

The dogs <u>will</u> run away if you leave the door open.

I told <u>you</u> I was going to win.

<u>Do</u> we know how many people are coming?

Practice

A Say each sentence and then listen to the recording. Circle the function words that have been reduced to schwa. Listen again and check your answers.

1. Be sure to pack a suit and tie for the trip.
2. Colin doesn't know when we can leave.
3. Hard times will have that effect on people.
4. The chef forgot to put salt and pepper in the dish.
5. How do I reach the manager?
6. He refused to tell you the secret, didn't he?
7. What are you doing for dinner?
8. My sister can give them a discount.
9. Everyone will need a paper and pencil.
10. They can speak French and German.

The Prominence of Stress

In speech, you can stress different words to modify the meaning of what you say. The same sentence said in different ways can have a slightly different meaning depending on the specific words that are emphasized; this use of stress clarifies the exact meaning of the sentence to the listener.

Take the sentence *Artists often make sacrifices for their work*. Read three different ways, this sentence has slightly different meanings. Listen to it read three times and pay attention to how the stressed word in each example makes the exact meaning more precise in each case.

- **Artists** often make sacrifices for their work.
  (One type of person that might have to make sacrifices to pursue their work is artists.)

- Artists **often** make sacrifices for their work.
  (Artists don't occasionally make sacrifices for their work; they do it all the time.)

- Artists often make **sacrifices** for their work.
  (Often, artists don't make a lot of money for their work; their commitment to their art takes personal sacrifice.)

Practice

A Listen to the sentences and circle the stressed word in each sentence. Then choose the emphasized meaning based on the word stress.

1. Sherry took a picture of Ben and his dog.
   a. Sherry's action was "took."
   b. Sherry took the picture, and not someone else.
   c. Sherry took a picture, and not something else.

2. Sherry took a picture of Ben and his dog.
   a. The picture also showed Ben's dog.
   b. The dog belongs to Ben.
   c. Sherry's picture also showed Ben.

3. I put two magazines in the desk drawer.
   a. There are going to be more magazines.
   b. The magazines belong to me.
   c. There are two magazines only.

4. I put two magazines in the desk drawer.
   a. The magazines' location is a drawer.
   b. I didn't do anything besides put the magazines in the drawer.
   c. The magazines are inside a drawer in a specific piece of furniture.

5. Yesterday he rode the bus to school.
   a. The bus only came yesterday.
   b. The day was yesterday, not any other.
   c. He didn't drive; he rode the bus.

6. Yesterday he rode the bus to school.
   a. The school was his destination.
   b. He rides the bus to work sometimes.
   c. The school is near the bus stop.

7. My daughter drew that beautiful picture on the refrigerator.
   a. I'm talking about my daughter's picture, not another picture.
   b. I'm talking about my daughter, not my son.
   c. I'm talking about my daughter, not other people's daughters.

8. My daughter drew that beautiful picture on the refrigerator.
   a. I think the picture is gorgeous.
   b. The picture is that one, not others.
   c. The picture is on the refrigerator, not on the wall.

9. The flight normally leaves at 7:30 in the morning.
   a. The flight leaves at 7:30, not sooner.
   b. The flight is a morning flight.
   c. The morning is the usual time the flight leaves.

10. The flight normally leaves at 7:30 in the morning.
    a. The flight usually leaves at this time, but sometimes it's late.
    b. The plane leaves, not the bus.
    c. The flight departs at 7:30; it does not arrive.

Intonation in Tag Questions

 A **tag question** consists of a statement and a question structure added to the end of the statement. The statement portion of the tag question normally uses falling intonation. The tag can use either rising or falling intonation depending on the speaker's meaning.

- **Rising intonation** in the tag indicates that the speaker <u>thinks</u> the statement is true, but he or she isn't certain. In other words, the speaker is asking a real question.

- **Falling intonation** in the tag indicates stronger certainty in the truth of the statement. The speaker is not asking a true question so much as anticipating agreement.

Below are two sentences that use **rising intonation** in the tag. Listen carefully to the intonation in each example. Note that it <u>rises</u> on the tag because the speaker is truly seeking an answer.

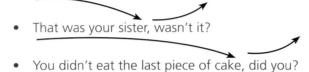

- That was your sister, wasn't it?

- You didn't eat the last piece of cake, did you?

Below are the same two sentences, but with falling intonation in the tag. Listen carefully to the intonation in each example. Note that it <u>falls</u> on the tag because the speaker is anticipating agreement.

- That was your sister, wasn't it?

- You didn't eat the last piece of cake, did you?

Practice

A Listen to the recording and then repeat the sentences. Then decide if the speaker is asking a true question or anticipating agreement. When you are done, check answers with a partner. Then take turns asking the questions.

1. You're Adele's cousin, aren't you?   **question / agreement**
2. That's the same jacket as mine, isn't it?   **question / agreement**
3. There are over a dozen people in the group, aren't there? **question / agreement**
4. They shouldn't have told him, should they?   **question / agreement**
5. You remembered to reschedule the meeting, didn't you? **question / agreement**
6. He's got a unique sense of humor, doesn't he?   **question / agreement**
7. You went to the party last night, didn't you?   **question / agreement**
8. Eating bananas makes you sleepy, doesn't it?   **question / agreement**
9. They were both born in November, weren't they?   **question / agreement**
10. You brought the present, didn't you?   **question / agreement**

B Write two tag questions: one that asks for an actual answer and another that expects agreement. Read your questions to a partner using the correct intonation. Then ask your partner which type of tag question it is.

1. _____

2. _____

Language Summary

Unit 1

adapt to change ideas or behavior in order to deal with something successfully **adaptable** (adj.)

clarify to explain something in order to make it easier to understand **clarification** (n.) **clarity** (n.)

collaborative done by two or more people working together **to collaborate** (v.) **collaboration** (n.)

conflict a serious argument about something important

convey to express a thought or feeling so that it is understood **conveyance** (n.)

detect to find or discover that something is present **detector** (n.) **detectable** (adj.)

distinct noticeably separate or different **distinctly** (adv.) **distinctive** (adj.)

document to record the details of an event **document** (n.) **documentation** (n.)

ebb and flow come and go **to flow** (v.)

endure to continue to exist **endurance** (n.) **enduring** (adj.)

ensure to guarantee

factors something that affects an event, decision, or situation

impulsive doing and saying things suddenly without thinking about it carefully **impulsively** (adv.) **impulse** (n.)

knowledge information and understanding about a subject **knowledgeable** (adj.)

landline phone traditional or home phone

linguist a person who specializes in the study of languages **linguistics** (n.) **linguistic** (adj.)

possess to have or to own **possession** (n.) **possessive** (adj.)

preservation protection (for the future) **(to) preserve** (v., n.)

remark something that you say (fact or opinion) **to remark** (v.) **remarkable** (adj.)

sensitive showing an understanding of others' feelings **sensitivity** (n.) **insensitive** (adj.)

slave someone who is the property of another person **to enslave** (v.) **slavery** (n.)

switch to change

threatened endangered **to threaten** (v.) **threat** (n.)

vanish to disappear

whine to complain in an annoying way about something unimportant **whiney, whiny** (adj.)

Unit 2

affluent wealthy **affluence** (n.)

broke having no money

budget a plan that shows how much money you have and how much you can spend **to budget** (v.)

cheapskate a person that does not like to spend money

credit a method that allows you to buy things and pay for them later

debt money that you owe **debtor** (n.)

disposable income the extra money you have left over after all your bills are paid

economist a person who studies the way in which money is used in society **economy** (n.) **economic** (adj.)

entrepreneur a person who starts his or her own business **entrepreneurial** (adj.)

fair deal a good business arrangement

headache a big problem

impact to have an effect on someone or something **impact** (n.)

loan money you borrow or lend **to loan** (v.)

make ends meet to keep one's expenses within one's income

materialistic valuing money and possessions very highly **materialism** (n.)

my treat it's on me; to pay for another's food or entertainment

nest egg money that you save for a particular purpose

on the house without charge; free

pay back to return money that you owe someone

profit money that is earned in business minus expenses **nonprofit** (adj.) **profitable** (adj.)

run out (of something) to have no more of something

sacrifice to give up something valuable to help yourself or others **sacrifice** (n.)

save up (for something) to put aside money for future use **savings** (n.)

snowball to increase rapidly

splurge to spend a lot of money on something, usually something you don't need

stability a situation that is calm and not likely to change suddenly **stable** (adj.) **unstable** (adj.)

terms the parts of the contract that all sides must agree on (e.g., how much a loan is for, how long one has to pay it back, etc.)

thrifty careful with money

value to attach importance to something **to undervalue** (v.) **value** (n.) **valuable** (adj.)

Unit 3

ban to refuse to allow **ban** (n.)

chaotic in a state of complete disorder **chaos** (n.)

community a group of people that live in a particular place **communal** (adj.)

cosmopolitan full of people from many different countries

dense containing a lot of people or things in a small area; crowded **densely** (adv.) **density** (n.)

descendants people of later generations

destruction the state of being destroyed **to destroy** (v.) **destructive** (adj.)

district an area of a town or country

drought a long period of time in which no rain falls

dynamic full of energy

global affecting all parts of the world; international **globally** (adv.)

immigrant a person who moves permanently to a different country **to immigrate** (v.) **immigration** (n.)

in isolation (from) separately (from) **to isolate** (v.), **isolated** (adj.)

infrastructure the basic facilities (such as transportation, power supplies, and buildings) that allow a city or organization to function

inhabitant person who lives in a particular place **habitable** (adj.) **uninhabitable** (adj.)

livable suitable for living in

manageable able to be dealt with easily **to manage** (v.) **unmanageable** (adj.)

metropolitan relating to a large, busy city **metropolis** (n.)

nutrition the foods that you take into your body (and how they influence your health) **malnutrition** (n.) **nutritious** (adj.)

per capita (the amount) per person

rapid fast **rapidly** (adv.)

renewal the act of restoring **to renew** (v.)

soil the substance on the surface of the earth in which plants grow; dirt

stunt to prevent something from growing as much as it should **stunted** (adj.)

transformation a complete change in the appearance of something (usually for the better) **to transform** (v.) **transformative** (adj.)

urbanization the process by which more and more people move from rural areas to the cities **suburban** (adj.) **urban** (adj.)

Unit 4

affectionate loving and warm **affectionately** (adv.) **affection** (n.)

ambitious very motivated to succeed **ambition** (n.)

be hard on (someone) to treat someone in a severe or unkind way

bully using one's strength or power to hurt or frighten others **bully** (n.)

correlate to have a close connection to something else **correlation** (n.)

demanding difficult; insisting that something be done your way **to demand** (v.)

get along (with someone) to have a friendly relationship with someone else

idealistic hopeful; believing in the best **idealism** (n.)

innovative creative; original; inventive; new **to innovate** (v.) **innovator** (n.)

lab partner in a science class like biology or chemistry the student you work with in the laboratory to do certain experiments or exercises **laboratory** (n.)

longevity long life

obesity the state of being very overweight **obese** (adj.)

picky critical; hard to please; choosy

pushover a person who is easily influenced by others **to push around** (v.)

reserved keeping one's own feelings hidden

safety net money you can rely on if you get into a difficult financial situation

sedentary inactive; sitting a lot

sensible logical; realistic **commonsense** (n.) **nonsense** (n.)

stubborn inflexible; unwilling to change your mind **stubbornly** (adv.) **stubbornness** (n.)

supportive helpful and kind to those in need **(to) support** (v., n.)

tax incentive a decrease in the amount of tax one must pay, which allows one to do something else **incentivize** (v.)

thorough careful; detailed **thoroughly** (adv.) **thoroughness** (n.)

tolerant accepting and open-minded **to tolerate** (v.) **tolerance** (n.)

unplug to relax and do nothing

upbeat positive and cheerful **downbeat** (adj.)

wear the pants to be in control or the main decision maker (used to describe a person)

work (something) out to find a solution to a problem

zeal a strong enthusiasm for something **zealously** (adv.) **zealot** (n.)

Unit 5

absorb to reduce the force of something; soak up or take in **absorption** (n.) **absorbent** (adj.)

aggressive acting in an angry or violent manner **aggressively** (adv.) **aggression** (n.)

amber a hard yellowish-brown substance used to make jewelry **amber** (adj.)

archaeologist a person who studies people and societies of the past by examining their culture, architecture, tools, and other objects **archaeology** (n.)

Bronze Age the period of ancient human culture between 4000 and 1200 BCE

bury to place something in a hole in the ground and cover it with dirt **burial** (n.)

case a situation or incident

cemetery a place where the bodies or ashes of the dead are buried

clue something that helps you find the answer to a problem **clueless** (adj.)

complex a group of buildings designed for a particular purpose

exotic very different or unusual

geological related to the study of the Earth's rocks, minerals, and surface **geology** (n.) **geologist** (n.)

infection a disease caused by germs or bacteria **to infect** (v.) **infectious** (adj.)

kudos public admiration or recognition received when doing something

loot to steal from shops and houses **loot** (n.) **looter** (n.)

monument a large structure, usually made of stone, built to remind people of something

mystery something that is difficult to understand or explain **mysteriously** (adv.) **mysterious** (adj.)

narrow down to limit or restrict **narrowly** (adv.) **narrow** (adj.)

observation the act of carefully watching someone or something **to observe** (v.)

oxygen a gas in the air that all humans, animals, and plants need to live

profile a set of data that shows the important characteristics of someone or something **to profile** (v.)

settlement a place where people gather to build homes and live **to settle** (v.) **settler** (n.)

skeleton the frame of bones supporting a human or animal body **skeletal** (adj.)

solve to find an answer to a problem or crime **to resolve** (v.) **unsolved** (adj.)

speculate to guess about something's nature or identity **speculation** (n.) **speculative** (adj.)

surroundings the immediate area around you **to surround** (v.)

theory a formal idea that is intended to explain something **theoretically** (adv.) **theoretical** (adj.)

tow to pull something or someone by a rope tied to a vehicle

twist to turn **to untwist** (v.) **twisty** (adj.)

uncover to discover something previously unknown or hidden **to cover** (v.)

unharmed not hurt or damaged in any way **(to) harm** (v., n.) **harmful** (adj.)

withstand to survive or not give in to a force or action **to stand up to** (v.)

Unit 6

atmosphere layer of air or gas around a planet **atmospheric** (adj.)

cutting-edge the most advanced or most exciting in a particular field

divergence separating; drawing apart **to diverge** (v.) **divergent** (adj.)

drawback aspect of someone or something that makes them less acceptable

efficient able to do tasks successfully without wasting time or energy **efficiently** (adv.) **efficiency** (n.)

feasible possible **feasibility** (n.) **unfeasible** (adj.)

gravity the force that causes things to drop to the ground **gravitational** (adj.)

green to make habitable for plant and animal life **green** (adj.)

habitable good enough for people to live in **to inhabit** (v.) **uninhabitable** (adj.)

innovative creative; original; inventive; new **to innovate** (v.) **innovation** (n.)

inspire to encourage or make someone want to do something

interact (with) to communicate as you work or spend time together with others **interaction** (n.) **interactive** (adj.)

obsolete no longer necessary because something better has been invented

primitive simple; not well developed **primitively** (adv.)

revelation very surprising or very good **to reveal** (v.)

take (something) for granted to accept that something is true or normal without thinking about it

versatile able to be used for many different purposes **versatility** (n.)

Unit 7

accomplish to achieve something or succeed at doing something **accomplishment** (n.) **accomplished** (adj.)

aptitude ability to learn a type of work or activity quickly and do it well

book smarts what you learn from books in school **street smarts** (n.)

common sense a person's natural ability to make good judgments and behave sensibly **sensibly** (adv.) **sensible** (adj.)

diabetes an illness in which someone has too much sugar in their blood **diabetic** (n., adj.)

excel to be very good at doing something **excellent** (adj.) **excellence** (n.)

have what it takes to have the background or skills necessary to do something

instinct the natural tendency of a person to behave or react a certain way **instinctively** (adv.) **instinctive** (adj.)

intellectual someone who studies a lot and thinks about complicated ideas **intellectually** (adv.) **intellect** (n.)

master someone who is extremely skilled at a particular activity **to master** (v.)

narrow down to remove items from a list so that only the most important ones remain **narrowly** (adv.) **narrow** (adj.)

nonsense silly or untrue **nonsensical** (adj.)

objective neutral; based only on facts **objectively** (adv.) **subjective** (adj.)

outcome a result or effect of an action or situation

stereotype the general idea that one has about an entire group of people **to stereotype** (v.) **stereotypical** (adj.)

strategy planning the best way to gain advantage or achieve success **strategically** (adv.) **strategic** (adj.)

street smarts the quick-thinking ability to handle difficult or dangerous situations, especially in big cities **book smarts** (n.)

vow to make a promise to oneself or another **disavow** (v.) **vow** (n.)

work out to find a solution to a problem

Unit 8

adore to feel great love and admiration for someone

appealing pleasing and attractive **to appeal (to somebody)** (v.) **unappealing** (adj.)

background the kind of work, life, and family experience you have

celebrated famous and much admired **celebrity** (n.)

commemorative officially remembering a famous person or major event **to commemorate** (v.) **commemoration** (n.)

cultivate to try hard to develop something or make it stronger **cultivation** (n.)

doable possible to do

exorbitant a price or fee that is higher than it should be **exorbitantly** (adv.)

exposure public attention that a person, company, or product receives **to expose** (v.)

flock to to go to a particular place or event because it's interesting, usually in large numbers

icon an important symbol of something **iconic** (adj.)

invest to put time or money into something because you think it will be beneficial **investment** (n.)

merchandise goods that are bought and sold in trade **merchant** (n.)

nominal very small **nominally** (adv.)

notorious to be well known for something bad **notoriously** (adv.) **notoriety** (n.)

paparazzi photographers who follow celebrities, photograph them, and sell the pictures

personable pleasing in appearance or manner **unpersonable** (adj.)

pitch (an idea) to persuade people to accept an idea **pitch** (n.)

remarkable unusual or special in a way that gets attention **to remark** (v.) **remarkably** (adv.)

renowned to be well known for something good **unrenowned** (adj.)

socialite a person who attends many fashionable, upper-class social events

status an accepted or official position

transition the process in which something changes from one state to another **transitional** (adj.)

Unit 9

addicted unable to stop doing something or consuming a certain substance **addictive** (adj.) **addiction** (n.)

alleviate to make easier to put up with **alleviation** (n.)

automatic doing something without having to think about it **automatically** (adv.)

bark the wooden material on the outside of the tree

boost to increase **boost** (n.)

botanical related to plants

burnout exhaustion at an early stage in life or career **to burn out** (v.) **burned-out** (adj.)

chronic constant; nonstop **chronically** (adv.)

cranky irritable, in a bad mood **crankiness** (n.)

crash to suddenly run out of energy and feel very tired **crash** (n.)

derive to receive or obtain from a source **derivation** (n.) **derivative** (adj.)

disrupt to prevent something from functioning in its normal way **disruption** (n.) **disruptive** (adj.)

distracted not focused because you are thinking about other things **to distract** (v.) **distraction** (n.)

drowsy sleepy **to drowse** (v.) **drowsiness** (n.)

habit something that you do regularly, often without thinking about it **habitually** (adv.) **habitual** (adj.)

heal to make or become healthy **healing** (adj.) **unhealed** (adj.)

herb a plant used for making medicine **herbal** (adj.)

incentive something that encourages you to act a certain way

leukemia a cancer of the blood

merge to combine

morning person a person who likes to get up early and is typically at his/her best during the morning hours

neuron brain cells **neurological** (adj.)

night owl a person who likes to stay up late

power through (informal expression) to use all your energy and will to accomplish something, often quickly, despite difficulties **power** (n.) **powerful** (adj.)

prescription a paper on which a doctor writes an order for medicine **to prescribe** (v.)

prone having a tendency to be affected by something, usually in a negative way

recover to become well again **recovery** (n.)

reinforce to support or make something stronger **reinforcement** (n.)

REM deep, dreaming sleep

remedy a medicine or treatment that cures or relieves

resilience the strength and ability to recover quickly from something bad **resiliency** (n.)

revert to go back to an old habit or way of doing something **reversion** (n.)

routine a habit, something you do regularly at the same time **routine** (adj.)

sleep deprivation a serious lack of sleep **to deprive** (v.)

sleep through (something) to continue sleeping without waking up **to oversleep** (v.)

substitute to replace one thing for another thing **substitution** (n.) **substitute** (n., adj.)

synthetic produced artificially **synthetically** (adv.)

toss and turn to keep turning around in bed because you cannot sleep

turn in to go to bed

willpower self-discipline; strong determination to do something **willfully** (adv.) **willful** (adj.)

Unit 10

a drop in the bucket a very small amount

accumulate to collect something together over time **accumulation** (n.)

adequate enough **adequately** (adv.)

algae plants with no stems or leaves that grow in water

astonishing very surprising **to astonish** (v.) **astonishment** (n.)

boil to produce bubbles of vapor in liquids when heated

carry out to put something into action

conserve to use something carefully so it lasts a long time **conservation** (n.) **conservationist** (n.)

contaminate to make something dirty or harmful **contamination** (n.)

dub to name

dwindle to decrease in number **dwindling** (adj.)

epic very large and impressive

evaporate to cause a liquid to change to a gas **evaporation** (n.) **vapor** (n.)

faucet a device that controls the flow of water from a sink or bath; the tap

freeze to turn a liquid into a solid **frozen** (adj.)

freshwater water that is not salty

glide to move in a quiet and smooth way **glide** (n.)

have access to (something) to have something available to see or use **accessible** (adj.)

in hot water in trouble

indigenous belonging to the place or country where something is found; native **indigenous** (n.)

lava hot liquid rock that comes out of a volcano

let off steam to release one's repressed emotions

Maya, the a civilization based in southern Mexico and northern Central America that prospered from 600 BCE to 900 CE

melt to change from a solid to a liquid state usually through heat

mercury a silver-colored liquid metal that is used in thermometers

mineral a natural substance usually obtained from the ground **mineral** (adj.)

mist large number of tiny water droplets in the air, which creates a kind of fog **misty** (adj.)

mouthwatering something very appetizing in appearance, aroma, or description

muddy covered with mud; not clear or pure **to muddy** (v.) **mud** (n.)

plunge to move suddenly downward

potable suitable for drinking

pour to flow or cause to flow (a liquid)

propel to push or move something forward

purify to make something clean **purification** (n.) **pure** (adj.)

restore to return something to its original (usually better) state **restoration** (n.)

run to let flow

rust a brown substance that forms on metals that come in contact with water **rusty** (adj.)

saturate to soak **saturation** (n.)

scarce limited, in short supply **scarcity** (n.)

seep to flow slowly and in small amounts (liquids and gases) **seepage** (n.)

shortage a lack of something

sinkhole a hollow place or depression that collects water

sip to drink little by little **sip** (n.)

soak to wet something completely; to saturate

spill to accidentally flow from a container **spillage** (n.)

symbiosis relationship between two different organisms that benefits both **symbiotic** (adj.)

take the plunge to do something decisively especially after a period of hesitation

tap faucet

toxic poisonous **toxicity** (n.) **nontoxic** (adj.)

underworld the place where spirits of the dead live

vast extremely large **vastly** (adv.) **vastness** (n.)

water under the bridge events that are past and done with

Unit 11

accent (color) a secondary color used to emphasize **to accent** (v.)

breakthrough an important development or achievement **to break through** (v.)

commissioned to be formally arranged to work for someone **commission** (n.)

design to plan and draw an object so that it can be built or made **designer** (n.)

faulty not made correctly or not working properly

fixated thinking about something to an extreme and excessive degree **fixation** (n.)

frustrated feeling upset or angry because you are unable to do anything about a problem **to frustrate** (v.) **frustration** (n.)

genius a highly talented, creative, or intelligent person **ingenious** (adj.)

graffiti words or pictures that are drawn in public places

hollow having space inside it (as opposed to being solid all the way through)

impasse a difficult situation in which further progress is not possible

in a flash (happening) suddenly and for a very short time

inscription something written by hand in/on a book, photograph, or painting **to inscribe** (v.)

insight a clear, deep, and sometimes quick understanding of something complex **insightful** (adj.)

intense very great or extreme in strength or degree **intensely** (adv.) **intensive** (adj.)

logo special visual design or writing of a company's name that is used on products and advertising

masterpiece an extremely good painting, novel, movie or other work of art

mural a large picture painted on a wall **muralist** (n.)

priceless worth a large amount of money **price** (n.)

slogan short phrase that is easy to remember

stage part of an activity, process, or period

tranquility a peaceful, calm state **tranquil** (adj.)

vandalism deliberate damaging of things, especially public property **vandalize** (v.) **vandal** (n.)

wander to stray in movement or in thought

Unit 12

comedian entertainer who tells jokes to make people laugh **comedy** (n.) **comedic** (adj.)

contagious spreads quickly among a group of people **contagion** (n.)

coping mechanism an action or effort intended to relieve stress **to cope** (v.)

delivery the way a joke or humorous story is told **to deliver** (v.)

exaggerate to indicate that something is bigger, worse, or more important than it really is **exaggeration** (n.)

expose uncover, reveal **exposure** (n.) **unexposed** (adj.)

hilarious extremely funny

hysterical extremely funny

in good/bad taste fitting (or not fitting) generally accepted social standards

kid to say something as a joke

let one's guard down to relax

off-color rude or offensive

offensive something that upsets or embarrasses because it is rude or insulting **to offend** (v.) **offense** (n.)

parody a piece of work that makes fun of an original work (painting, book, movie, song, etc.) **to parody** (v.) **self-parody** (n.)

point out to direct attention to something

practical joke a prank **to joke** (v.)

prank a trick played on someone often with the goal of slightly embarrassing them

profanity offensive language; swearing **profane** (adj.)

punch line the words at the end of a joke that make it funny

shortcut a way that is more direct or quicker

social awkwardness feeling of embarrassment or difficulty in situations **awkwardly** (adv.) **awkward** (adj.)

stereotype to unfairly characterize all members of a certain group (ethnicity, nationality, gender, age, etc.) as being the same **stereotype** (n.) **stereotypical** (adj.)

universal relates to everyone in a group, society, or the world **universally** (adv.)

witty amusing in a clever way **wit** (n.)

Grammar Summary

Quantifiers

General amounts	Specific amounts (within a group)
Quantifiers describing general amounts are followed by plural count nouns and noncount nouns.	Quantifiers that describe specific amounts are followed by singular count nouns (except *both* and sometimes *each*).
All students have cell phones.	**All members of a group**
A lot of students call their parents after school.	**Each/Every student** has a cell phone.
They spend **a lot of time** on their phones.	**Each of **** the **students** has a cell phone.
There are **many students** studying English.	**Any student** in this class can converse in English.
Quite a few students speak English well.	
Some students need help with their homework.	**Talking about two things**
I have **some free time** and can help you.	The meeting will be on Monday or Tuesday.
A few* students study other foreign languages.	**Both** days** are fine with me.
We don't have **much time** to study for the exam.	**Either day** is fine.
None of the **students** like homework.	**Neither day** works well for me.
**Another common expression with *few* is *very few* (which is an even smaller amount).*	*****Each of** and **both** are followed by a plural count noun.*

large amount →

nothing →

Much is not used alone in affirmative statements. Use *a lot of* instead: ~~She has much time~~. She has a lot of time.

Note that when *each* is the subject, the verb is singular. When *none* is the subject, the verb can be either singular or plural depending on the situation. For example:

*None (not any) of the translators **speak** French.*
*None (not one) of the translators **speaks** French.*

Noun Clauses

noun clauses starting with *that*	I like this jacket. How much is it?
	I think **(that) it is $50**.
noun clauses starting with a *wh-* word	I like this jacket. How much is it?
	I don't know **how much it is**.

Some **noun clauses** begin with the word *that*.
Other **noun clauses** begin with a *wh-* word (*who, what, where, why, how, when, which, whose*). These clauses follow statement word order even though they start with a question word.

Certain verbs are commonly followed by a noun clause . . .
• verbs that describe an opinion, feeling, or mental state: *assume, believe, guess, forget, hope, know, remember, suppose, think, understand, wonder*
• verbs that describe something someone said: *admit, explain, mention, say, tell*

Notice! In everyday spoken English, sentences that use verbs such as **assume**, **believe**, **guess**, **hope**, **suppose**, **think** can often be shortened using *so* instead of writing the full noun clause.
Q: *Can we afford a new laptop?*
A: *I think so.* (i.e., *I think that we can afford a new laptop.*)

Q: *Are you getting a good grade in this class?*
A: *I hope so!* (i.e., *I hope that I am getting a good grade in this class.*)

The negative form for *I guess/suppose/hope/think so,* would be:
I guess/suppose/hope not.
I don't think so.

Some noun clauses end with a period, and some end with a question mark. If you're making a statement, end with a period. If you're asking for feedback or suggestions, end with a question mark.

Grammar Summary

A noun clause is a dependent clause that acts like a noun in a sentence. For example, a noun clause can be used as a subject or an object of a verb.

> I don't know **why he borrowed so much money**.
> **Why he borrowed so much money** is really confusing to me.

Noun clauses can also follow adjectives.

> I'm not **sure** what to do.

Unit 3

> **Notice!** The form for the dynamic and stative passive is the same: a form of *be* + the past participle.

Dynamic and Stative Passive

Dynamic Passive	Stative Passive
Belize City, the former capital, **was** nearly **destroyed** by a hurricane in 1961. The government **was moved** to Belmopan in 1970.	Belmopan, the new capital, **is situated** inland on safer ground, but Belize City **is** still **known** as the financial and cultural center of the country.
• This form of the passive expresses an action. The focus is on the receiver of the action, not the performer. • Use *by* + agent to name the performer of the action. (We don't use a *by* phrase when the performer is unimportant, unknown, or is obvious.) • The past participle functions more like a verb than an adjective. It expresses the action.	• This form of the passive describes a state or condition. • Because there is no action being expressed, it's impossible to name the agent. • Instead, we use a form of the passive followed by a preposition (not necessarily *by*). • The past participle functions more like an adjective than a verb. It describes the subject.
Verbs used with dynamic passive: *built, created, destroyed, divided, moved, sent*	***Verbs used with stative passive:*** *acquaint (with), associate (with), cover (with), crowd (with), dress (in), involve (with), know (as), made (of), situate (on)*

Unit 4

Making Wishes

> For *be*, use *were* with both singular and plural subjects. In everyday spoken English, *was* is also used.

	Real Situation	Ideal Situation
❶ **about the present**	I**'m** kind of short.	I wish (that) I **were** taller.
	I **don't speak** French.	I wish (that) I **spoke** French.
	She **has to leave** the party now.	She wishes (that) she **didn't have to leave**.
❷ **about the past**	I **was** careless on the exam.	I wish (that) I **had been** more thorough!
❸ **with** *would*	We can't hear the teacher.	We wish (that) the teacher **would speak** louder so we could hear him.

Use *wish* to . . .
❶ talk about something you would like. In the *that* clause, the verb is in a past form.
❷ express regret about something that happened. In the *that* clause, the verb is in the past perfect.
❸ express displeasure in the moment with something or someone and to say that you want it to change.

The ideal situations can also be presented in a shortened form.

> I'm not very outgoing, but I wish (that) I were. (I wish I were outgoing.)
> I don't speak French fluently, but I wish (that) I did.(I wish I did speak French fluently.)

The difference between *wish* and *hope* can sometimes be confusing. When talking about a situation that is **present, hypothetical, but probably not possible**, use *wish*.

> *I wish (that) I were rich.*

Note that the verb in the *that* clause takes a past form (were).

When talking about a **possible future** situation, use *hope*.

> *I hope (that) I get into Stanford University!* (NOT: *I wish (that) I get into Stanford University.*)

Note that the verb in the *that* clause is often in the present tense.

Unit 5

Modals of Possibility in the Past, Present, and Future

	Present/Future	Past
strong certainty	(9:45 a.m.) Joe's not here yet. He **must** be on his way, though.	(9:45 a.m.) Ann's not here yet. She **must have** left her house late.
weaker certainty	(9:50 a.m.) He's still not here. He **could/may/might** be stuck in traffic.	(9:50 a.m.) She's still not here. I **could have/may have/might have** told her the wrong time.
impossibility	(9:58 a.m.) He just got here. I **can't/couldn't** be more relieved.	(the next day) Ann said she didn't see me at the zoo. She **couldn't have** looked very hard—I was there the whole time!

Unit 6

Predictions with Future Forms

future continuous: Use to show that an event will be ongoing in the future.	*will/be going to* + *be* + present participle ❶ In five or ten years, robots **will be functioning** in human environments.
future perfect: Use to show that a future event will be finished by some future point in time.	*will* + *have* + past participle ❷ By 2020, scientists believe that we **will have found** a cure for certain types of cancer.
future in the past: Use to talk in present time about a prediction that was made in the past.	*would* or *was/were going to* + base form of the verb Carlos thought getting a job after graduation **would be** hard, but he was hired by a company right away.

❶ It would also be correct to use the simple future or *be going to* here. Notice though that the simple future states that an action will or won't happen. The future continuous emphasizes the duration or ongoing status of the action.

❷ This sentence means that at some point before 2020, scientists will discover a cure for cancer. It would also be possible to say here, *We will find a cure for cancer by 2020*.

Noun Clauses with *Wh-* Words and *If/Whether*

wh- clauses	Combine a *wh-* question and a statement. Change the question to statement word order.
	She taught sixty students in one class. How does she do it? → *I don't know how she teaches sixty students in one class.*
if/whether clauses	Combine a *yes/no* question and a statement.
	Did he pass the exam? I wonder. → *I wonder if/whether he passed the exam (or not).*
	If and *whether* are often interchangeable, but they are not quite the same. Use *if* when the noun clause outlines one condition. Use *whether (or not)* when the noun clause states alternative possibilities, whether explicitly stated or implied.
	*Let Anne know **if** Jack is coming.* (Anne only needs to be contacted if Jack is coming.)
	*Let Anne know **whether** Jack is coming.* (Anne needs to be contacted whether he comes or not.)

 TIP You can add *or not* immediately after *whether*. *I wonder whether or not he passed the exam.*

Many, but not all, of these will be used in the negative when forming the *wh-* or *if/whether* clauses:

- not certain
- forget*
- have no idea
- don't know
- can't remember

- don't see (= don't understand)
- not sure
- can't tell (= can't figure it out)
- don't understand
- wonder*

*Do not use the negative.

Examples:

I'm not certain how many students study abroad every year. Do you have any idea?

I can't remember/I forget exactly what the minimum TOEFL score is, but it's probably over . . .

I can't tell what the most efficient way to study is because it's different for each person. For me, I like to . . .

I wonder if a good education guarantees a good job. My cousin went to an excellent university, but he's having trouble finding work.

The phrase "whether or not" has a second meaning that is different than the usage in the chart. It can also mean "regardless." For example:

I want to go to the school with the best reputation, whether it is expensive or not!

Unit 8

Reported Questions

Quoted Speech	Reported Speech
Yes/no questions: Are you going to win an award?	❶ They asked him **if he was going to win an award**. They asked him **whether (or not) he was going to win an award**. They asked him **whether he was going to win an award (or not)**.
Are you getting tired of the paparazzi?	She asked him **if he was getting tired of the paparazzi**.
Wh- questions: Who are you here with?	❷ He asked him **who he was there with**.
Where are you going?	They wanted to know **where he was going**.

❶ Notice how the verb forms change (backshift) in reported questions.
❷ Notice the shift from *here* to *there*.
❸ You can use the expression *want to know* in place of *ask*.

> Backshifting doesn't occur when . . .
> • the question is a general truth/ regular occurrence or habit,
> • the speaker repeats something that was just said, or
> • when the reporting verb is in the present tense.

Unit 9

Stating Conditions: Other Ways of Expressing *If*

Conditions	Meaning
❶ I can take a break **(but) only after/only if** I study for an hour. I can take a break **provided that/as long as** I study for an hour.	I can take a break if (and only if) I study for an hour.
❷ I'll be sleepy **unless** I have a cup of coffee first.	I'll be sleepy if I don't have a cup of coffee first.
❸ You should set your alarm. **Otherwise**, you won't wake up on time in the morning.	If you don't (set your alarm), you won't wake up on time.
❹ I wouldn't join that gym, **even if** you gave me a free membership.	Nothing can make me join that gym, even a free membership.

❶ The words in bold express that one thing must happen first (studying) in order for another thing to happen (taking a break). Note that expressions with *only* can be preceded by *but*.
❷ *Unless* introduces a condition (having coffee) that will prevent a possible outcome (being sleepy).
❸ After a suggestion (set your alarm), *otherwise* shows what the result will be if the person does not follow the suggestion (you won't wake up on time).
❹ *Even if* is used when a result (I wouldn't join that gym) stays the same whether or not something else (you gave me a free membership) happens or is true.

The words and phrases in the chart can be used with present real or unreal conditionals. The examples in the chart can also be written as below.

> **Only if** *I study for an hour* **can I** *take a break*. (This is very formal language.)
> **Provided that/as long as** *I study for an hour, I can take a break*.
> **Unless** *I have a cup of coffee, I'll be sleepy*.
> **Even if** *you gave me a free membership, I wouldn't join that gym*.

Notice that these alternate structures do not apply to *otherwise*. It must follow the form in the chart.

Use *only if* with different conditionals to describe a more restrictive situation. If the sentence begins with the *if* clause, then the main clause is inverted.

> **We can** *cure the patients but only if we locate more medicinal plants*.
> *Only if we locate more medicinal plants* **can we** *cure the patients*.

Articles: *A/An*, *The*, and No Article (Ø)

a/an **vs.** **the**	Use *a/an* for count nouns in general or when we mention something for the first time. A: *Do you have* **a** *pen I can borrow?* (Any pen will do.) B: *Sure, here you go. When you're finished, just leave* **the** *pen on my desk*.
	Use *the* for specific nouns the speaker and listener already know about. *Can you turn off* **the** *faucet?* **The** *water is running*. (We both know these things.) *I think I left* **the** *car keys in* **the** *bathroom*.
the **vs.** **Ø**	Use Ø (no article) to talk about people or things in general. Use *the* to talk about particular people or things. *In parts of Africa, water is scarce*. *Most of* **the** *water we use is for cooking and bathing*.

Talking about Things in General

- Use <u>noncount nouns</u> (without *the*) to talk about people/things in general.
    We learned about **water** *in science class*.

- Also use <u>plural count nouns</u> (without *the*) to talk about people/things in general. In this case, it refers to all people.
    People *need access to clean water*.

- Use <u>singular count nouns</u> (with *a/an*) to talk about one example of a person/thing in general. In this case it means any single person.
    A person *needs access to clean water*.

- You cannot use <u>singular count nouns</u> (with *a/an*) to talk about all members of a group in general.
    ~~A dolphin should be protected.~~ **Dolphins** *should be protected*.

	Expressions That Use *the*	Expressions That Don't Need Articles
everyday life	• common experiences in our lives: *taking the bus, singing in the shower, reading the newspaper* Some common exceptions: *in bed, in class*	• certain everyday places: *in prison, during church, at work, at home, leave school* • certain pairs: *day after day, husband and wife, from top to bottom* • other fixed expressions: *by car, on foot, at sea, start college, by day, at night*
buildings and culture	• hotels, theaters, and museums: *the Oriental Bangkok, the Lennox Theater, the National Museum* • entertainment expressions: *listen to the radio, enjoy the play* exception: *appear on TV*	• names of most public institutions such as government buildings, train stations, airports, etc.: *City Hall, Union Station, JFK Airport, Times Square* exceptions: *the Bank of England, the White House*

Expressions That Use *the*	Expressions That Don't Need Articles
the environment and people	• our physical environment in general: *the weather, the mountains, the town* exceptions: ~~the nature~~, ~~the space~~ • oceans, rivers, and deserts: *the Indian Ocean, the Nile, the Sahara* • mountain ranges and island chains: *the Urals, the Seychelles* exceptions: single mountains and islands don't need an article: *Mount Everest, Hawaii*	• names of continents, countries, and states: *Africa, Jamaica* exceptions: (1) countries that are in plural form: *the Netherlands*; (2) countries that contain a noun like *republic* or *kingdom* in their name: *the People's Republic of China, the Kingdom of Saudi Arabia* • languages: *I speak Italian. French isn't easy to pronounce.* • the population as a whole: *Italians love to cook.* exceptions: nationalities that don't have a plural *-s* form: *The French make good movies. The Japanese celebrate many festivals.*
ordering and identifying	• ordinals and superlatives: *the second person in line, the longest river*	• after *a kind/sort/type of*: *a kind of challenge*

Unit 11

Adjective Clauses with Object Relative Pronouns		
	Describing People	**Describing Things**
❶ Restrictive clauses	The most creative person **who(m)/that/Ø** I know is my mother.	The computer **which/that/Ø** I use was obviously designed by a creative thinker.
❷ Nonrestrictive clauses	My best friend, **who(m)** I've known since childhood, is very creative.	This computer, **which** I bought last week, was obviously designed by a creative thinker.

> While *whom* is grammatically correct, in spoken English you will most often hear *who* in its place.
>
> Using *which* as a relative pronoun with restrictive clauses to describe things is grammatically correct, but in practice and usage *that* or no pronoun is generally used.

❶ These clauses give <u>necessary information</u> about the object. They complete the meaning of the sentence. In restrictive clauses you can also omit the relative pronoun: *The most creative person I know is my mother.* The relative pronoun *that* is only used with restrictive clauses.

❷ These clauses give <u>extra information</u> about the object. You don't need them to complete the meaning of the sentence. They are separated from the main clause by commas. You cannot omit the relative pronoun.

Unit 12

Tag Questions	
A tag question is a question added to the end of a statement. Tag questions are used to either confirm or query a conclusion. They often indicate the speaker's attitude about a topic.	
Tag questions include a pronoun and an auxiliary verb. They comment on a preceding statement.	**You haven't** read that, **have you**? **We laughed** so hard at that joke, **didn't we**? **You think** so, **do you**?
Affirmative statement + negative tag = the speaker assumes that the listener agrees. The anticipated answer is "yes."	**He's** really funny, **isn't he**? (Anticipated answer: *Yes, he is funny.*) **You'll** come to the show tonight, **won't you**? (Anticipated answer: *Yes, I will come tonight.*)
Negative statement + positive tag = the speaker assumes that the listener agrees with a negative point of view. The anticipated answer is "no."	**She isn't** a very good actress, **is she**? (Anticipated answer: *No, she isn't.*) **They couldn't** understand the joke, **could they**? (Anticipated answer: *No, they couldn't.*)
In other contexts, tag questions can be used to anticipate disagreement or an emotional response. See p. 165 of the Grammar Summary for more details.	

> You'll sometimes hear the ungrammatical expression *aren't I* in a tag question. This is common in casual speech.
>
> *I'm right, aren't I?*

Skills Index

Skills Index

Speaking

choosing the perfect celebrity to endorse your product, 92

convincing billionaire investor to loan money, 21

discussing restoration of vacation spot, 117

evaluating works of art, 129

explaining mysterious places in the world, 54

presenting a report summary, 10

sources of learning, 79

speaking about space exploration, 69

taking a life satisfaction survey, 45

talking about factors affecting physical and mental well-being, 105

talking about push/pull immigration factors, 34

telling a humorous story, 138

Speaking strategies

expressing an opinion, 17

interpreting the results, 10

making comparisons, 45

refuting a theory, 54

using pauses and emphasis, 138

Topics

art and creativity, 120–131

celebrity, 84–95

cities, 24–35

exploration and the future, 60–71

health, 96–107

humor, 132–144

language, 1–11

learning and education, 72–83

money, 12–23

mysteries, 48–59

personality, 36–47

water, 108–119

Videos

Borrowing Money, 20

Climate Change Drives Nomads to Cities, 32

Discoveries in a Village Near Stonehenge, 55

A Hidden Language Recorded, 8

How Your Brain Handles Stress, 104

The Immigrant, 139

Jellyfish Lake, 116

Profiles in Exploration, 70

The Secrets of Long Life, 44

In the Spotlight: Kate Middleton, 93

Student Voices on University Rankings, 78

Urban Art: Graffiti, 128

Vocabulary

animal mysteries, 50, 154–155

bad health, healthy solutions, 98, 156–157

cities of the world, 26, 153

comedy of Jerry Seinfeld, 134, 157

communication, 2, 152

creative problem solving, 122, 157

famous people, 86, 156

intelligence, 74, 155–156

personality description, 38, 153–154

robot revolution, 62, 155

spending habits, 14, 152–153

water, 110, 157

Writing

comparing and contrasting yourself with another person, 46

counterarguments, 68–69

definition essay, 130

describing an important life lesson, 82–83

describing cause and effect, 106

e-mail for formal communication, 118–119

explaining advantages and disadvantages, 22

opinion piece containing facts and opinions, 94–95

persuasive essays, 142

recounting a story, 58

report summary, 9–10

summary, 33

Writing strategies

balancing facts and opinions, 94

definition essay, 130

guidelines on summary writing, 33

making a counterargument, 68

report summary, 10

showing cause and effect, 106

thesis statement and conclusion, 82

using a graphic organizer to tell a story, 58

using appropriate register, 118

Credits

Photo Credits

Unit 1 **pp.x–1**: Tim Pannell/Corbis; **p.2**: Cindy Hughes/Shutterstock.com; **p.4**: Rachel Frank/Corbis; **p.5**: Digital Vision/Thinkstock; **p.6**: Christopher Pillitz/In Pictures/Corbis; **p.7**: Randy Olson/National Geographic Stock; **p.8**: UIG via Getty Images; **p.11**: D. Hurst/Alamy

Unit 2 **p.12–13**: Marin Tomaš/Demotix/Corbis; **p.14** left: PhotoAlto/Alamy, right: Tomas Rodriguez/Corbis; **p.15**: Chris Collins/Corbis; **p.16** top: Andre van der Veen/Shutterstock.com, bottom: ©iStockphoto.com/97; **p.17**: Michael Melford/National Geographic Stock; **p.18**: ©iStockphoto.com/drbimages; **p.19** top: Karen Kasmauski/Corbis, bottom: Atlantide Phototravel/Corbis; **p.20**: Datacraft Co., Ltd./Corbis; **p.21** Tetra Images/Corbis; **p.23**: Image Source/Corbis

Unit 3 **pp.24–25**: Songquan Deng/Shutterstock.com; **p.26**: Murat Taner/Getty Images; **p.27**: Kazuko Kimizuka/Getty Images; **p.28**: Paulo Fridman/Corbis; **p.29** top: Atlantide Phototravel/Corbis, below: Aaron Amat/Shutterstock.com; **p.31**: Greg Girard/National Geographic Stock; **p.32** top & below: MORANDI Bruno/Hemis/Corbis; **p.34**: Florian Werner/Getty Images; **p.35** top & bottom: Jane Sweeney/JAI/Corbis

Unit 4 **pp.36–37**: Radius Images/Corbis; **p.38** top: Brooke Whatnall/National Geographic Stock, bottom: Kimberly White/Reuters/Corbis; **p.39**: vipflash/Shutterstock.com; **p.40**: Frederic Cirou/PhotoAlto/Corbis; **p.41**: Zigy Kaluzny–Charles Thatcher/Getty Images; **p.43**: Topic Photo Agency/Corbis; **p.44**: David Sutherland/Getty Images; **p.45**: Lawrence Manning/Corbis; **p.46**: Tim Pannell/Corbis; **p.47** top: Rubberball/Mike Kemp, bottom: Ocean/Corbis

Unit 5 **pp.48–49**: Agustin Esmoris/National Geographic My Shot; **p.50** top: Arman Taylo/National Geographic My Shot, below: Mitsuaki Iwago/Minden Pictures; **p.51**: Tim Fitzharris/Minden Pictures; **p.52**: Ewan Burns/Corbis; **p.53**: Department for International Development; **p.54** left: Richard Nowitz/National Geographic Stock, right: Ocean/Corbis; **p.55**: National Geographic Maps/National Geographic Image Collection; **p.56** top: Atlaspix/Shutterstock.com, below: Layne Kennedy/Corbis; **pp.56–57**: Kenneth Geiger/National Geographic Stock; **p.59** left: Christoph Gerigk ©Franck Goddio/Hilti Foundation, right: Sergey Kamshylin/Shutterstock.com, donatas1205/Shutterstock.com

Unit 6 **pp.60–61**: Image Source/Corbis; **p.62** top: Kirsty Wigglesworth/AP/Corbis, bottom: Oliver Killig/epa/Corbis; **p.64**: MCT via Getty Images; **p.65**: Peter Ginter/Science Faction/Corbis; **p.66**: NASA; **p.67**: Art by Stefan Morrell. Sources: Christopher McKay, NASA Ames Research Center; James Graham, University of Wisconsin -Madison; Robert Zubrin, Mars Society; Margarita Marinova, California Institute of Technology. Earth and Mars images: NASA; **p.69**: NASA – digital version copyright/Science Faction/Corbis; **p.70** top: Maria Stenzel/National Geographic Stock, bottom: Tyrone Turner/National Geographic Stock; **p.71**: Sigrid Olsson/PhotoAlto/Corbis

Unit 7 **pp.72–73**: Karen Kasmauski/National Geographic Stock; **p.74**: Louie Psihoyos/Corbis; **p.76**: Jon Hicks/Corbis; **p.77** top: Blue Jean Images/Corbis, bottom: mirrorimage photos/Demotix/Demotix/Corbis; **p.78**: Paul Hardy/Corbis; **p.79** top: Hill Street Studios/Blend Images/Corbis, bottom: Catherine Karnow/National Geographic Stock; **p.80–81**: Russ Schleipman/Corbis; **p.81** top: Getty Images; **p.82**: Lisa Stokes/Getty Images; **p.83**: David Arky/Corbis

Unit 8 **pp.84–85**: Ocean/Corbis; **p.86**: Splash News/Corbis; **p.87**: moodboard/Corbis; **p.88**: Condé Nast Archive/Corbis; **p.89** top: Splash News/Corbis, bottom: Splash News/Corbis; **p.90**: OMEGA/epa/Corbis; **p.91**: Atlantide Phototravel/Corbis; **p.92** left: Richard Cohen/Corbis, center: Pulse/Corbis, right: Matthias Kulka/Corbis; **p.93**: WireImage/Getty Images; **p.95**: AFP/Getty Images

Unit 9 **pp.96–97**: Dawn Kish/National Geographic Stock; **p.98**: @erics/Shutterstock.com; **p.100**: Sandra Seckinger/Corbis; **p.101** top: Frederic Cirou/PhotoAlto/Corbis, middle: Bloomimage/Corbis, bottom: Timurpix/Shutterstock.com; **p.102**: Lynn Johnson/National Geographic Stock; **p.103** top: Pete Oxford/Minden Pictures/Corbis, bottom: Kevin Schafer/Minden Pictures; **p.104** top: Dawn Kish/National Geographic Stock, below: Joel Sartore/National Geographic Stock; **p.105**: John Lund/Sam Diephuis/Blend Images/Corbis; **p.106**: Fancy/Alamy; **p.107**: Mark Thiessen/National Geographic Stock

Unit 10 **pp.108–109**: Ben Welsh/Design Pics/Corbis; **p.110**: Wolfgang Langenstrassen/dpa/Corbis; **p.111**: Michael St. Maur Sheil/Corbis; **p.112**: David Kadlubowski/DIT/Corbis; **p.114**: Annie Griffiths/National Geographic Stock; **p.115** top: Macduff Everton/Corbis, bottom: Krista Rossow/National Geographic Stock; **p.116** top: Bob Krist/Corbis, below: Ingo Arndt/Minden Pictures/Corbis; **p.117**: Elnur/Dreamstime.com; **p.118**: Atlantide Phototravel/Corbis

Unit 11 **pp.120–121**: Tibor Bognár/Corbis; **p.122**: Konstantin Sutyagin/Shutterstock.com; **p.124**: Klaus Tiedge/Corbis; **p.125** top: jbk–editorial/Alamy, bottom: Cameron Davidson/Corbis; **p.126**: The Gallery Collection/Corbis; **p.127**: Alinari Archives/Corbis; **pp.128–129**: Mike Kemp/In Pictures/Corbis; **p.129** left: Corbis, middle: Seattle Art Museum/Corbis, right: Nano Calvo/ZUMA Press/Corbis; **p.130**: Mafe/Corbis; **p.131**: Chris Hill/National Geographic Society/Corbis

Unit 12 **pp.132–133**: Melissa Brandts/National Geographic My Shot **p.134**: Charles Rex Arbogast/AP/Corbis; **p.135**: ©iStockphoto.com/Lichtblick1968; **p.136**: Rich Legg/Getty Images; **p.137** top: Mike Watson/moodboard/Corbis, bottom: Asterisco.org/Corbis **p.138** top: I Love Images/Corbis, bottom: Tim Davis/Corbis; **p.139**: CinemaPhoto/Corbis; **p.140**: Matilda Hartman/Corbis; **p.141**: Scott Stulberg/Corbis; **p.142**: Paul Hardy/Corbis **p.143**: MM Productions/Corbis

Text Credits

Readings from the following units were adapted from National Geographic.

Unit 1 Adapted from *What Happens When a Language Dies?* by Paroma Basu, National Geographic Extreme Explorer, February 26, 2009. **Unit 2** Adapted from *Nobel Peace Prize Goes to Micro-Loan Pioneers* by Stefan Lovgren, National Geographic Traveler, October 13, 2006. **Unit 3** Adapted from *The City Solution* by Robert Kunzig, National Geographic Magazine, December 2011. **Unit 4** Adapted from *Secrets of the Happiest Places on Earth* by Ford Cochran, National Geographic NewsWatch, November 22, 2010. **Unit 5** Adapted from *Bejeweled Stonehenge Boy Came From Mediterranean?* by Kate Ravilious, National Geographic News, October 13, 2010. **Unit 6** Adapted from *Making Mars the New Earth* by Robert Kunzig, National Geographic Magazine, January 15, 2010 and *Q&A: Robert Zubrin, Mars Pathfinder* by Ted Chamberlain, National Geographic ADVENTURE, September/October, 2000. **Unit 9** Adapted from *Nature's Rx* by Joel Swerdlow, National Geographic Magazine. **Unit 10** Adapted from *Water World* by Stuart Thornton, National Geographic, Education Beta, July 13, 2010. **Unit 11** Adapted from *Lost Leonardo da Vinci Mural Behind False Wall?* by Dave Mosher, National Geographic News, March 12, 2012.

the **WORD**
among us®
The *Spirit* of Catholic Living

This book was published by The Word Among Us. Since 1981, The Word Among Us has been answering the call of the Second Vatican Council to help Catholic laypeople encounter Christ in the Scriptures.

The name of our company comes from the prologue to the Gospel of John and reflects the vision and purpose of all of our publications: to be an instrument of the Spirit, whose desire is to manifest Jesus' presence in and to the children of God. In this way, we hope to contribute to the Church's ongoing mission of proclaiming the gospel to the world so that all people would know the love and mercy of our Lord and grow more deeply in their faith as missionary disciples.

Our monthly devotional magazine, *The Word Among Us*, features meditations on the daily and Sunday Mass readings and currently reaches more than one million Catholics in North America and another half-million Catholics in one hundred countries around the world. Our book division, The Word Among Us Press, publishes numerous books, Bible studies, and pamphlets that help Catholics grow in their faith.

To learn more about who we are and what we publish, visit us at www.wau.org. There you will find a variety of Catholic resources that will help you grow in your faith.

Embrace His Word, Listen to God . . .

www.wau.org

Bibliography

She Reads Truth Bible. Nashville: Holman Bible Publishers, 2017.

The Didache Bible with Commentaries Based on the Catechism of the Catholic Church.
    San Francisco: Ignatius Press, 2015.

The Navarre Bible: New Testament Expanded Edition. New York: Scepter Press, 2008.

Hahn, Scott, general editor. *Catholic Bible Dictionary*. New York: Doubleday Religion, 2009.

Hahn, Scott, editor, and Curtis Mitch, compiler. *Ignatius Catholic Study Bible: New Testament*.
    San Francisco: Ignatius Press, 2010.

Houselander, Caryll. *Wood of the Cradle, Wood of the Cross: The Little Way of the Infant Jesus*.
    Sophia Institute Press, 1995.

Krugh, Karen Lynn. "Seeing Christ in All People." www.catholicculture.org. 2016. Accessed
    February 2, 2016, https://www.catholicculture.org/culture/library/view.cfm?recnum=528.

L'Engle, Madeleine. *Walking on Water: Reflections on Faith and Art*. New York: Convergent Books,
2016.

Lewis, C. S. *The Weight of Glory: And Other Addresses*. San Francisco: HarperOne, 2001.

Above All is a Lenten devotional journal that includes daily Scripture passages (set in context with enlightening historical notes to deepen your understanding), as well as devotional essays, room to journal, and space to organize your time. There is a simple prompt for the ancient prayer form of *lectio divina* each day, as well as a separate page for the fifth stage, *Actio*, where the reader is encouraged to examine her conscience and offer forgiveness to herself and to others. *Above All* is designed to help you reflect on all aspects of your life, particularly those that you may have pushed to the back burner. It's filled with tools to help you discover which areas need greater care and tending, and is meant to inspire and motivate you to become your absolute truest self, so that come Easter, you can flourish as God intended. The entire study—both words and images—is carefully crafted so that women can share it with the men in their lives, too.

Flourish

To the people of Rome, the cultural center of the world at the time, St. Paul wrote the most comprehensive expression of the gospel. For us, the Book of Romans is a study of sin and guilt, loss and rescue. It is the essential gospel. An in-depth look at the entire Book of Romans, this study provides inspiration and structure to dig deeply into St. Paul's guidebook for the early Church—and for us who are the Church today.

Hosanna

Hosanna is a Lenten devotional journal that is a deep and wide study of the Gospel of Matthew. Each weekday, readers will find a simple prompt for journaling tuned to the heart of the ancient prayer form of *lectio divina*. Weekends are reserved for rest and for hiding his word in the hearts of those who love him. *Hosanna* is designed to help you reflect on all aspects of your life in light of Jesus' call to live for the kingdom of heaven. It's at once gentle and challenging—a journey with one of Jesus' closest followers that will bring you into the presence of our Lord, from his birth to his resurrection.

Ponder

An intimate encounter with the Rosary, this lovely volume integrates Bible study, journaling, and thoughtful daily action prompts. You will grow in your appreciation and understanding of the beautiful, traditional Rosary devotion, while deepening your love for Jesus in the Gospels.

Ponder for Kids

Created especially for children, this book contains Bible stories for every mystery of the Rosary. Full of interesting things to do, the journal is bursting with discussion questions, personal prayer prompts, puzzles, and coloring pages. There are also nature study pages to create a botanical rosary.

Stories of Grace

Here you will find thirty-one days of Jesus' stories carefully collected for you. Along the way, we've provided meditation essays, journaling prompts, space for your notes and drawings, beautiful calligraphy pages, and prayers to draw you deeper into the parables Jesus told. Do you have eyes to see and ears to hear our Lord's stories of grace?

Rooted in Hope

A newly revised bestseller, *Rooted in Hope* is a thirty-three-day Advent and Christmas study that extends from November 30 to January 1. In a look at Scriptures that tell the stories of prominent biblical figures, this study echoes and expands upon the popular Advent tradition of a Jesse tree. For each day, you'll find Scripture, a devotional essay, pages for guided *lectio divina*, and space to organize your days. Journaling pages and useful planning pages feature clear and elegant design, exquisite hand-drawn illustrations, and gorgeous calligraphy. A handy companion for Advent and Christmas seasons, this book will become a treasured keepsake for the woman who uses it.

True Friend

Whether we are nineteen or forty-nine, friendship with other women can enrich our lives and it can make us weep. How do we find friends who are kind and true? By becoming those friends ourselves! This beautiful book invites you to explore what God has to say about lasting friendships.

Call Me Blessed

Every day of this four-week study provides Scripture to get you started and notes for further Bible reading. Step by step, day by day, biblical reading and inspiring essays introduce you to nineteen women of the Bible whose stories bring to life the dignity and vocation of women of God throughout the ages. Consider the stories of these biblical women in the light of the gospel, and see how their truths beckon you to also become a woman of God.

Consider the Lilies

Specifically designed to be an encouragement when times are tough, this six-week study provides Scripture to get you started and notes for further Bible reading. You will find a daily devotion, some thoughts to consider as you journal, and a prayer prompt to dovetail with your reading. Step by step, day by day, these words console and bring clarity to the hard days. Maybe this is a difficult season in your life—you're overwhelmed by the burdens weighing you down, the crosses the the Lord has asked you to carry. This study is for you. It is full of the consolations of the Holy Spirit. Here, you will find a guidebook to what God is saying, how he is encouraging you to lament, to pour out your grief and your fears and your anger. Or maybe you're in a sweet spot. Life is really rather good right now. This study is for you, too. It makes you a better friend to the woman next to you, to the growing child who aches, to the spouse who despairs. And it buries words in your heart so that they are there, waiting, when the rain begins to fall. Because it will fall.

Allison McGinley recently moved to the Philly suburbs with her husband and two kids, and is living her dream with a church, library, and diner within walking distance. She returned to her faith during college, and nothing has been the same ever since, in the best way. Writing is the way she processes life and discovers the beauty all around her, and she's been known to write in her closet in the middle of the night when the right words were suddenly found. She's happiest when taking photos of beautiful things, worshipping God through song, drinking a cup of coffee, or standing by the ocean.

Kendra Tierney believes that anything worth doing is worth overdoing. To that end, she has nine kids (so far), literally wrote the book on liturgical living in the home, and, in her spare time, is renovating the family's hundred-year-old Los Angeles-area home. Her favorite parts are the Adam and Eve-themed laundry closet—after all, laundry is their fault—and the cathedral-ceilinged attic storage room that she's converted into a home chapel, complete with donated pews, as well as stenciled ceiling, floor, and walls. She hopes to be done before the baby moves out.

Kate Wicker is a wife, mom of five, author, speaker, and a recovering perfectionist. She loves reading, running, shoes, God, and encouraging women to embrace the messiness of life instead of trying to cover it up, making excuses for it, or feeling ashamed of their brokenness or their home's sticky counters. From her home in Athens, Georgia, Kate strives every single, imperfect day to strike a balance between keeping it real and keeping it joyful.

Kristin Foss is a self-taught artist, plant person, minimalist wannabe, and ENFP (who appreciates intimate gatherings). She loves a good street taco second to a loaded poke bowl, but most nights she's at home sharing a homemade dinner with her family. She gravitates toward bright, vibrant colors and everything feminine and joyful. She believes home is a priceless place, and there are no rules to your heart's idea of aesthetic beauty.

Rebecca Frech is a big-mouthed girl who comes from a long line of opinionated women. She's a Texas girl who smokes a mean brisket and is always happy to show off her smoke rings. A self-proclaimed history nerd, she bought the house behind the town library in order to support her book-a-night reading habit. When she's not cooking, gabbing, or reading, she spends her free time raising eight children, remodeling her historic home, and sneaking off to the gym to lift all the things!

Mary Haseltine is a thirty-something wife, mom, doula, and author who writes about motherhood, birth, babies, miscarriage, doulaing, marriage, faith, and any other deep thoughts that strike her fancy. She's a passionate lover of Jesus, Scripture, the Church, JPII's Theology of the Body, and her husband and six boys. When not swimming in a sea of testosterone, she can be found working with doula clients, escaping from the house for a (quiet!) coffee and writing session, or enjoying a much-needed glass of wine with girlfriends. She lives in an old farmhouse in western New York with a flock of chickens and a whole lot of dreams.

Meg Hunter-Kilmer is a hobo missionary who lives out of her car and travels around the world giving talks and retreats; in her heart, though, she lives in a house surrounded by lilacs in a small town in the South and spends her afternoons on the front porch with a stack of Young Adult princess books and a plate full of pastries. That not being an option, she spends much of her time making small talk, listening to audiobooks, and hunting down unlocked churches where she can make a holy hour. She hates bananas with a burning passion and used to keep a guitar pick in her wallet just in case—despite the fact that she doesn't play guitar.

Mary Lenaburg relishes entertaining. Her door is always open and the coffee hot. When traveling to speak, she loves to explore the local candy shops looking for the perfect dark chocolate fudge (with nuts is best). Mary spends her free time reading the latest best-selling murder mystery and baking her famous chocolate chip cookies, ensuring that the kitchen cookie jar is always full. Mary and her husband have been happily married for thirty years, finding joy among the ashes, having lost their disabled daughter, Courtney, in 2014. They live in Northern Virginia with their grown son, Jonathan.

Contributors

Rachel Balducci is a book author, newspaper columnist, television talk show cohost, and a university communications professor. Her favorite mission, however, is being a wife and a mom. Rachel and her husband, Paul, have five sons and one daughter, and lately life with boys involves lots of food and lots of basketball. Rachel writes about the intersection of faith and family, and she thinks often about how cleaning her bathroom will make her a saint.

Colleen Connell is a bringer-upper-of-boys and wannabe saint who packs a little Louisiana spice with her wherever she goes. She currently serves at-risk families in her job as a social worker in Fort Wayne, Indiana, and spends copious hours on football and soccer fields yelling more loudly than all the other moms. She finds joy in the word, the world, and the wild wonder of everyday life.

Katie Curtis grew up in Chicago but moved to the East Coast in high school, and now lives in Portsmouth, NH with her giant Scottish husband and six kids (including one-year-old twin boys). A Midwest girl at heart, she loves her neighbors, coffee, and conversations that get deep. When she isn't writing or cooking, she is driving her kids to sports or getting gummed on by babies. Her ideal day includes a writing session, a Rosary, a run, a dance party with her kids, and everyone home for a yummy dinner.

Micaela Darr is a California girl, born and raised, with brief stints in Mexico, Spain, and South Korea. She's extroverted by nature, but being a mom of seven kids has driven her to appreciate having quiet alone time, too. Her husband, Kevin, is the best in the world, especially because he's exceedingly patient in regards to her harebrained schemes (see: living in South Korea). Micaela is disorganized by nature, but is also bound and determined to improve herself in that area and has done so with a modicum of success. She loves to read, watch good TV, and chat your ear off.

Elizabeth Foss is a morning person who relishes her time alone with the word as much as she loves the inevitable interruption by the first child to wake. There is something so hopeful about every new day! A wife, mother, and grandmother, she's happy curled up with a good book or tinkering with a turn of phrase. She alternates between giving up coffee and perfecting cold brew. Elizabeth would rather be outdoors than inside, and she especially loves long walks in the Virginia countryside that sometimes break into a run.